Toni
Thanks
a $ Million
for the kind
words.
Jim Voris

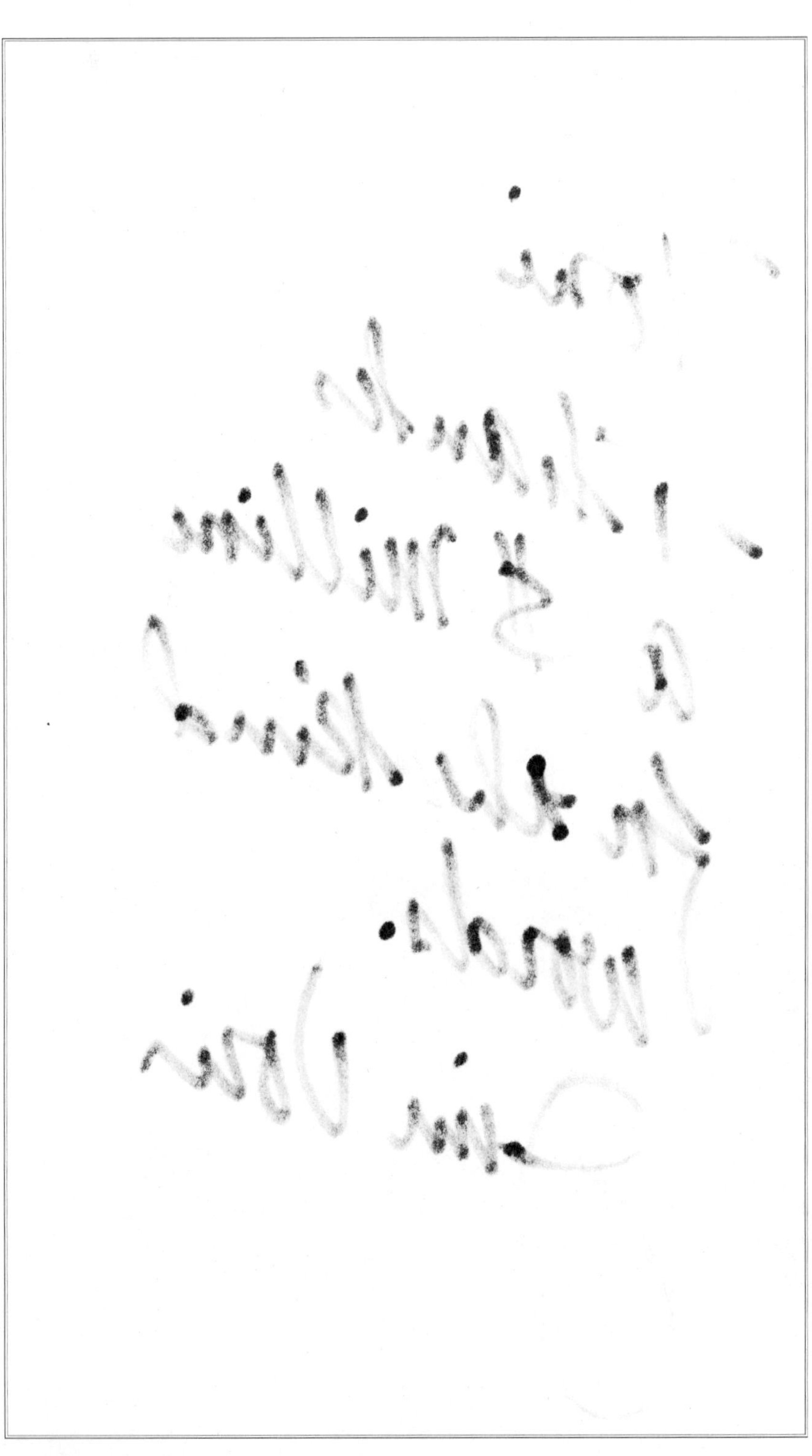

Helluva Ride

A whimsical look at the life and times of a US Air Force Photographer in the 50's/60's

BY

JAMES LEE VORIS

Disclaimer

This book is work of fiction. All names, places, and incidents are the product of the author's imagination and/or used fictitiously. Any similarity or resemblance to any actual persons, living or dead, business establishments, events, or locales are entirely coincidental.

Published by LULU Press

BOOK ID: 11744439 (soft cover)

www.lulu.com

ISBN 978-1-4709-2486-7

First Edition

Visit Author's website at www.jamesleevorisbooks.com

Covers, title page & internal art designed and all photographs by James Lee Voris

Dedication

To all the loving spirits and memories to me betide. A special thanks to Melanie, my lovely wife and patient editor, for all her wonderful help and support. An extra special wave and wink to all the great folks named. Without them, there would be no great memories.

Ω

Helluva Ride

Life and times of an Air Force Photographer

Table of Contents

BAF (Before the Air Force)

All the following snippets of my life's adventure are absolutely true, well, … as time and seas may mellow. Truth is, as you get older, the memory tends to smooth over some stuff you no longer recall with absolute certainty (*to sworn truth in a court of law*) and stories do tend to get better with the ripening. That said, nothing has been "made up" or, on purpose, embellished unless it contains a disclaimer, or some such warning, that the author may be a tiny bit fuzzy on the full truth of the matter. With that understanding aside, as author, I claim the right to take certain editorial license to add a little tweak or comment, if the humor of the moment calls for it.

Following High School graduation and a fun summer, I entered the USAF (*October, 1958*). Oh wait, before I get into the Air Force bit I should mention I was a CAP (*Civil Air Patrol*) cadet. I had my Certificate of Proficiency and was the Cadet Commander of our Squadron (*Springfield Squadron 702*). CAP is an Auxiliary of the USAF and with a Certificate of Proficiency you could enter the Air Force with your first stripe. You still went to Basic Training, but you started one pay-grade up and one rank above the other basic trainees. It wasn't a gift to get the Certificate of Proficiency, you had to earn it. You learned the elements of flight, Search and Rescue, Military Customs and Courtesies, drill marching, and I think you had to have logged so many hours of "observer" flying time as well. In addition you needed at least two, 2 week encampments at an Air Force Base (*CAP Camp*) that I found out later was "more demanding" than the actual Basic Training in the Air Force. (*But that is a whole other story.*)

I should also point out that prior to the entry into the USAF I worked 4 years for a professional photographer. He took me on the summer following my freshman year graduation (*Junior High School*). I say took me on, as I worked for him two full years for nothing, just to gain experience. (*Full time summers and afternoon and weekends during the school year.*) I told my Uncle (*Emil Voris*) that I wanted to be a photographer when I grew up. He said he knew a professional photographer and that I should go ask him if I could work for him "just for the experience." I was working for my Dad at the time who was the store manager of the Springfield Martin Rosenberger Wallpaper Company. I was making 35 cents an hour as the stock boy. As a result of my Uncle's suggestion, that very afternoon I walked out to the photographers studio. It was about twelve blocks from the wallpaper store and a hot early summer Saturday as I recall. On entry to George Wisler Commercial Photography Studio I remember stepping in from the hot street to the cool AC and in particular the smells of photo chemicals that would become such a part of my life. There was no one at the reception desk but a buzzer sounded when I entered. I waited for a while looking at the wonderful 16x20 pictures lining his reception area. Wedding pictures, portraits, industrial shots of gears and such, along with major local events like the big fire that nearly burned down the center core block of the city. Such a grand mix of photos that almost covered every aspect of life. If that wasn't enough to impress me what followed sure did. I waited about 10 minuted saying "Hello?" occasionally. I thought I heard voices coming from the back so finally braving trespassing I entered the back area, announcing myself as I proceeded. When I entered the actual studio area I discovered this photographer standing at a huge camera on a tripod focusing. On a french posing bench against a blue paper background was a beautiful lady (*about mid twenties I'd guess*) very scantly covered with a sheer drape. My jaw dropped and the photographer turned my way. He instantly stopped what he was doing and rushed to me saying, “Yes! What can I do for you?” as he ushered me back out to the reception area. I told him about Uncle Emil's suggestion and after giving me the quick look over said, “Okay, come back Monday, we'll talk then. I am kinda busy right now.” and directed me out the door. I heard the door lock as I hit the street. My eyes were dazzled from what I saw. I vividly recall saying to myself, *'Yes! Yes! This is exactly what I want to do the rest of my life.'*

That was my introduction to George Wisler and the wonderful world of professional photography. It was my third summer (*HS Junior*) that my father said that I had to find a real job that paid money. He said he would pay me 50 cents an hour at the wallpaper store. I announced to George that I had to quit. I wasn't gone a day when he called me and said, “Get you ass back here, I can't find a f__king thing. I'll pay you!” When I ask how much, he responded, “One dollar an hour!” I was in heaven and even dad couldn't complain about my getting paid. George was a great boss and he took time to explain things to me. Nomenclature was one of the first lessons. One day, early on when I was working for George for free, I was cleaning up and he told me to get him the “Strobe packs.” I asked what a strobe was and he jumped on me saying that if I expected to be a photographer I needed to know what everything is called. From that time on, as I would clean out this or that and come up with something I didn't know its professional nomenclature, I would ask. In the years to follow I never had an occasion when he asked me for something, I not only knew what it was and how it worked. Most important, as it turned out, I knew where it was.

One night as I was working late printing in the dark room, I realized it was almost 9:00pm and I was suppose to be home by nine. I came out of the lab area into the studio drying my hands and preparing to leave when I noticed the studio lights were all on. There on the famous french posing bench was a gorgeous nude woman. George was back at the camera and when he saw me he calmly said, "Lynda, this is Jim, my assistant."

She responded with a cute "Hi Jim." and stuck out her hand in anticipation of shaking hands. I hurriedly finished drying my hands and went to her with my hand extended. We shook hands, me standing there, holding the delicate, warm hand of this wonderful NAKED woman.

George broke the moment saying to me to "Come look at this." I retreated to the camera where he went into a lengthy discussion. "See how the light plays across her body creating the form?" He talked to me how posing was so important in creating the lines of composition. Despite the fact that I was 16 years old and this was the first fully naked woman I had ever seen in my life, he suddenly made it clinical and professional. I literally 'forgot' at the moment this was actually a naked woman in front of me. I listened intently to the explanations and soon he had me out adjusting lights and arranging props.

The phone rang at about 10pm and it was my Mom chewing me out. I explained that I was "helping George with a shoot and it could be a little while longer." She bought it, but warned me that in the future I had to call if I was going to be late. I think George dropped me at home near midnight. I said earlier that "I forgot - at the moment" that it was a real live naked woman I was looking at. That moment now passed and I really had wild dreams that night realizing what I had been doing. I can honestly say that throughout my photographic career it has never 'bothered' me to shoot nude women. I go into some kind of artistic mode and "see" only light and shadow as it plays on texture, shape and form to create a beautiful composition. I happen to believe there is nothing more beautiful than the nude female body the way God created it. That is not to say that I don't "react" later thinking about the beautiful lady I had shot. I always tried to make my pictures as "sexy" as possible promising everything but actually show nothing. I think I owe that to George's training.

One cold Saturday a lady named Snow that George hired as a printer (*It must have been about Fall 1956 and George was becoming quite successful and was hiring people.*) Snow complained that it was cold and asked me to go down in the basement and light the gas furnace. (*I never lit a gas furnace before!*) The basement of the studio was accessed by door in the floor with steps that went down to the dirt floor. One single 40 watt light lit the basement. I asked Snow what to do?

She said, "Find the thingy that turns on the gas and light the burner."

That sounds like ample instructions to me. I did find a flashlight and after careful examination I discovered there was a row of things that looked like burners deep inside the furnace and I was able to locate a valve associated with presumably the gas supply (*which was correct*). The burners were too far away to reach so I would need something long that was burning to reach them. I ask Snow to roll up a newspaper into a long thin tube. She did and still standing at the top of the stairs to the basement handed me my "ignition stick." I turned on the gas and using my zippo lighter (*I smoked then*) I lit the end and quickly shoved it in the furnace. It went out before I got it in. I guessed it really wasn't burning enough so I re-lite it. Once it was burning REAL GOOD – so it wouldn't go out - I carefully threaded it back into the furnace. Well I should say I started to thread it back into the furnace!

BOOM! There was an explosion! Something took hold of me and literally threw me across the basement up against the wall. Snow said from her vantage point all she saw was the basement enveloped in a red fireball. Later inspection showed two 2x12 beams were cracked.

Snow is screaming, "Jim, Jim are you alright!" I am in shock at what the hell happen. "Jim!" Snow shouts, "If you don't answer me I'm calling the emergency squad!"

"I'm okay, I guess!" I respond with a groan, got up and walked to the steps shaking my head. When Snow saw me she started laughing. Seems my eye lashes, eye brow's, and a quarter of the hair on front of my head had turned to ash. Oh, yeah, the furnace was lit by the way. My efforts had managed to also light the pilot. (*They didn't have all the safety features on furnaces back then!*)

I went with George on many of his fire calls and on one we were in the upstairs of an actively engaged fire, I'm handing him film holders when the fireman shouts "The roof is gonna cave in, get out of here!" I am closest to the door, and an outdoor staircase. I am going down the steps as fast as my little fat legs will go but George kept right behind me shouting faster, faster. So when I am about 8 steps from the bottom I vault over the railing to the ground to get out of the way of not only George but also the line of Fireman. **Bam**, I land on my feet, but in a pile of rubble of crap the fireman have pulled off the roof and walls. A nail sticking up off a board has penetrated my shoe and deep into my foot.

I decide to stand on the board and raise my impaled foot, thinking I can simply extract myself from the nail. What happens is I actually pull the nail from the board and it stays in my shoe. When I take the next step I finish driving the nail through my foot as well as the rest of the way through the shoe. The local radio station WBLY is covering the fire and the on scene remote unit volunteers to take the "only casualty" (*me*) to the hospital. I become the "on scene injury live interview" while we drive to the hospital. My mother just happens to be listening to the radio. She somehow beat us to the Hospital! Ohh, by the way, it hurts (*a LOT*) to extract a nail back through your shoe. It also hurts (*EVEN MORE*) to have an iodine soaked 27 mile long (*OK, I admit that may be some exaggeration*) gauze strip pulled back through where the nail had passed.

Okay. I promise, just one more story with George...

One early afternoon in September 1957 (*just before I went into the Air Force*) I was working in the studio and George's fire monitor went off saying there is an explosion at Rockway Elementary School. George screams to quick grab all available loaded film holders, and camera bags and in a dead run we were out the door. George drove a 1957 Buick that went flat out. We went through town with the horn blaring and lights flashing, careening around corners sometimes on two wheels, burning rubber. We came upon two highway patrol cars. (*Rockway Elementary School was a country school*) The OHP cars had their lights and sirens flashing but they were going too slow for George so he passed them. We arrived about the same time as some fire equipment and emergency vehicles were pulling in. George skidded to a stop but put the car out of the way of the all the arriving emergency equipment. As we leaped out George shouted, "Bring the film and stick with me like glue!" We raced inside the burning building where George shot pictures of the fire fighters extinguishing overhead flames and into a class room to take pictures of rescuers extracting a teacher from under her desk. When it was over and we were back outside, one of the Ohio Highway Patrolman said to George, "You were kinda speeding coming out here, wouldn't you say, George?"

George offhandedly answered, "What was holding you guys up, it was an emergency?"

"Ahh, we were going as fast as the patrol car could go George, 120 mph!" Was the Officers response.

I don't know to this day how fast we were going but we passed them like they were standing still!

Anyway, enough pre-history, … on with the saga!

USAF Boot Camp

I notified my Air Force Recruiter in early July of 1957 that I wanted to delay my scheduled enlistment date from the first of October to the Spring of '58. This was because I had been awarded an CAP-ICE (*Civil Air Patrol–International Cadet Exchange*) trip to the Antarctica to participate in the Geo-Physical Year - Operation Deep Freeze. They scheduled me to go in late October and it would be at least a 3 month stay. I was very excited about it as it was one of the top National ICE awards, certainly the longest deployment. It was really a big thing that Antarctic summer of 1957-58. I hadn't actually signed any papers that made me official USAF property yet, but my Recruiter made it sound like I didn't have a choice. He indicated I had to fulfill my "obligation" and meet my scheduled (*voluntary*) enlistment date. *(I found out later that was total BS and that he was just to lazy to try working schedules around me. As I said, I didn't actually belong to the Air Force yet and I should have said, "Fine, then I won't join up!" If I had, he most certainly would have relented and worked with me rather than lose an enlistment.)* So, … a decision I have regretted all my life, I turned down the award and met my scheduled enlistment date.

Because I was already an E-2 (*Single stripe– A/3c*) the recruitment center put me in charge of the new recruits for our trip to San Antonio, Texas (*Lackland AFB*). We flew out of Columbus Ohio on a late night flight. It was a commercial airline (*I don't recall the Company Line*) and had real Airline Stewardesses. Being "in charge", I was in the back seat and the two Stewardess (*All very pretty females in those days. This was before all the Affirmative Action - when it became law that being ugly and cantankerous got better treatment than being good looking and pleasant.*) Well it was a fun trip and while everyone else was sleeping I was partying with the Stewardesses. Fun while it lasted. When we arrived in San Antonio it was still dark, well before a new day would peek over the horizon.

We were met by screaming T.I.'s (*Technical Instructors*) that was to be the way of life for the next 8 weeks. I handed the manifest list of all the men on my flight to a screaming T.I. He took it and promptly order me, "Airman Puke, to fall in with the rest of the maggots." He began to rattle off the names on the list and directed us to a bus as our names were called. We were to shout "HERE SIR" as the name was called and run for the bus. Most of the new recruits didn't know what I had garnered from my CAP encampment experiences. The main objective of military Basic Training is to gain unquestioning compliance to what ever stupid thing they might come up with. When my name was called I screamed at the top of my lungs (*it was loud – very loud as I had a good set of lungs*) "HERE SIR!" and was on the bus before the sound reach the T.I. (*Okay that may be a slight embellishment!*) But I did run faster than anyone else and it made an impression. On the bus the T.I. said to me "What branch were you in prior to transferring to the Air Force?" assuming, I suppose, I might be a Army or Navy crossover. I told him proudly, "CAP Sergeant!" (*Note: technically you don't call a enlisted grade NCO, 'Sir', so I followed Military Customs and Courtesies and called him what he was, a Sergeant!*) He looked at me like I just told him I was a Russian spy and said "What fu_kin country is that?" I never saw that T.I. again so I obviously wasn't in his flight.

Air Force P.T.

In the fall of 1957, there was an article in Argosy Magazine exposing the Air Force's supposed P.T. Program at Lackland AFB. It was a scam that every recruit was forced to endure. It went like this.

We arrive at Basic Training after an all night flight from wherever, and processed through the "Green Monster." (*The base personnel center was a huge central processing building where all personnel functions took place, from arrival to exits. It was painted green, hence the name "Green Monster".*) We were rushed thru a quick breakfast, then on the bus to our barracks where we were assigned a bunk and a footlocker. We were ordered to sit at attention on our footlocker at the foot of our bunk. After a couple hours of that the T.I. had everyone 'fall out' and explained this was P.T. day. A rag tag bunch of exhausted, civilian clothed new recruits were 'fast paced' (*Later to be called double time – marching but this was not by any stretch of the imagination any form of marching*!) to a mammoth field that had three (*or four - I don't recall*) football fields side by side. It was fairly well choreographed as the field filled up quickly. Then this "Adonis" of a brute that made Charles Atlas look like a wimp, leaps up on a platform and announces that "we" will do everything that he does. He proceeds to drop down and starts doing rapid push-ups. He is at about number 25 before the last of the bewildered field of men are even down on their bellies to start. T.I.'s are running up and down lines of men on the ground screaming orders that are incoherent to most. After Mr. Adonis does 100 push-ups, he rolls over and said we were now doing sit-ups. (*This was the days before crunches - this was a full sit-up.*) I think I had (*maybe*) done 8 push-ups when a T.I. is kicking me to roll over and start the sit-ups. I hear the guy on the platform calling sit-up number 36 when I have completed almost one full sit-up. Somewhere about my 5th sit-up, Superman announced 100! Then it was "Up, everyone up!" T.I.'s are screaming as we were now to start touching our toes. (*Ha! Never in my life, even to this day, have I been able to touch my toes with my legs straight. Something about my ham string just won't stretch that far.*) T.I.'s are screaming, guys are starting to pass out and I am stretching as hard as I can and I am reaching somewhere about halfway between my knees and my ankle when I hear the announcement "99 - 100! And now we do jumping jacks!" Somewhere in the haze of it all with me on about my 7th jumping-jack the Jock-man calmly finishes his count "98-99-100!" and said something to the extent that now we should be loosened up and can start our run. He leaps off the platform and shouts "Follow me!" He has made almost one full trip around the fields by the time all the rows of guys are even in a trailing line. He ran, T.I.'s just screamed orders at us and clapping hands saying to 'Pick it up', 'Go, go go!' 'Hurry up you pussy's, 'faster-faster'. Hercules had completed the 20th circle around the huge field before the last of us new recruits were down and out. He got back on the platform and said we were all pathetic examples of manhood and he said he would have to have much more PT with us to get us in shape. He hinted that today he was easy on us and we would have to pick up the pace next time. That planted the fear into our brains that even today I occasionally have nightmares about huge football fields.

Our T.I. had us fall-in and ranted and raved about what an embarrassment we were to him and that we were the worst of the whole group at the field. (*Of course I knew every T.I. was saying that to their Flight as well.*) He also said we were going to get 'extra P.T.' because we were in such bad shape. (*But you know, I didn't notice any of the T.I.'s doing the exercise routine! Humm?*)

By now it was lunch time and we attempted to march (*A staggered walk actually*) to the Chow Hall. We were all exhausted, sick to the point that several threw-up, and led through a chow line that most of the newbies were not prepared for. Rule was, if it's on your tray you eat it. The recruits pulling KP duty that passed out food saw us as fresh meat. (*Remember we were still in civies.*) The relatively good stuff they were very judiciously passing out. The stuff that was less than gourmet quality was heaped on the tray. If someone looked a bit green around the gills they loaded their tray knowing a T.I. would force them to finish their tray. You never said "I don't like … whatever" because that was an open invitation to get a triple helping. In fact a trick I used was to hint I really liked it (*For something I didn't care for*) and I was usually given a very small portion. For some reason the majority of the men failed to grasp this simple reverse psychology technique in the military. If they thought you liked something it was almost always denied to you.

Anyway, we were rushed through chow with a T.I. shouting and if you went up to turn your tray in, a T.I. was there to make sure it was a clean tray. If not, you were sent back to finished it. (*Note: I never had a problem with G.I. chow hall food and always found it wholesome and good. The only thing I ever had a little problem with was the vegetable soup. Not that it tasted bad, in fact it was almost always delicious. It was made from all the leftovers from the day before. On one occasion I had a piece of lemon pie in my vegetable soup and that is when I realized it really was garbage soup, … but good tasting and well balanced in all the healthy food groups as well and that even includes dessert.*)

Following our 'leisurely' lunch it was off to the supply depot to be issued uniforms. You all have seen movies about that fiasco so I won't bother explaining. With our bag of new clothes we drug our exhausted butts back to the barracks to drop it all off. Then back outside to begin instruction on the rudiments of drill commands, 'attention', 'parade rest', 'left face', 'right face', 'about face' and the marching commands of 'forward march', 'to the rear march', 'column left/right', 'right/left flank' and 'left/right oblique'. It was here I got to shine. It was quickly evident to my T.I. that I knew this stuff and was aware he had his eye on me. We had three T.I.'s assigned to our flight. One was a Technical Sergeant, one Airman First Class and one Airman Third Class.

We marched (*sort-of*) to the chow hall to get our supper and returned to the barracks near sunset. Relax? Not a chance. We were to sit at attention on the footlocker again (*This consisted of feet and knees together, back straight, shoulders back, face and eyes forward, no eye movement, no speaking.*) While we sat there in this very uncomfortable position the T.I.'s explained the process of making our bed to their satisfaction, the proper storage of our uniforms and personal items. Then we had a G.I. party! This consists of scrubbing the barracks down. It was a couple minutes before 9:00pm when the T.I. said the barracks was “still a filthy mess” but we needed to rest our sorry butts and told us to get ready for bed. I was never so happy to hear 'taps' over the million watt loud speaker just outside our barracks. I know my head hit the pillow, but that was the last thing I remember of that day.

The next morning we were ordered to fall out in our uniforms. I hadn't had the opportunity to buy my stripe or sew it on so I still was a slick sleeve as they called it. After chow the T.I. told us we were assigned to go to P.T. There was a groan and the mashing of teeth. Several guys were ready to "go over the hill" at that announcement but then the T.I. said, "There is an option available to you if you can afford it. You can elect to take your P.T. by going horse back riding, bowling, roller skating, or archery. Otherwise it's to the P.T. Field. He explained how much it cost to do these activities and having guys that showed him they had the money line up for the various activities. I was short of sufficient funds to do the activities and feared for the worse on the P.T. Field, just knowing it would be hell all over again, but had no other option. I was wishing I had been a bit more prudent in my spending coming down to basic training.

The few of us that were left that couldn't afford to go 'play' were ordered to fall in and we marched to the P.T. Field. A different place this time. It was a ball field and when we got there the T.I. got a bag of bats, gloves and balls and told us to play ball. He said he would be back in a couple hours to pick us up. We all looked at each other and wondered what the f_k was going on? So we played ball for a couple hours and when he came back we went to chow. Back at the barracks we sat around polishing shoes until the other guys returned. They bragged how much fun they had, some talking about the WAF recruit they met skating, or the horseback riders adventures, even a group ended up playing golf. All of us that were forced to stay behind agreed to keep it a secret about our 'day' at the P.T. Field and only said it didn't seem as bad this time as it was the first time. Every P.T. Day after that I went to the field and played ball except once I did go roller skating to see how the other half lived. It was fun, met some WAF's and that was more fun.

I started off saying there was an article in Argosy Magazine exposing the Air Force supposed P.T. Program. The article cover pictured recruits roller skating with the headline saying, "These Air Force recruits are receiving Physical Training at Lackland AFB!" (*or something to that extent.*) The article went on to expose the fact that the (*off base*) facilities of riding stables, bowling alley, skating rink, golf course and archery range were all owned by the Commanding General of the base and the first introduction of the recruits to P.T. was to instill a very strong motivation (*called fear!*) to do these other activities, even though it cost money to do them. I believe the article prompted an investigation and the practice was discontinued.

Stripe on

The first moment there was an opportunity to get to the base tailor I had my stripe sewn on each of my uniforms. It was done "professionally" so I knew it would be sewn on to AF specifications. The first time we "fell out" with my stripe on the T.I., at the moment, was the A/3c. As he walks the ranks he freezes when he gets to me. He looks at the stripe on my sleeve then up at me saying "What the hell is that on your arm, Airman?"

"Airman third class stripe, Airman Smith." (*That wasn't his real name, but I am sorry to say I don't recall his name*.) I responded, loud and clear, but stood at attention and still looking straight ahead.

"Get it off! That is an order!" He said.

"I am an Airman Third Class, and authorized to wear my proper rank, Airman Smith!" I responded, again loud and clear.

He spun around and mumbled something like "We'll see about that!" and left the whole flight standing there at attention as he went into the barracks. I suspect he went to check records and or see the top T.I., the Tech Sergeant. He returned shortly and called me to fall out of the ranks and come into the barracks. Which I did, but my feeling of security was starting to wain. Inside we went to the T/Sgt's office/quarters and the Sgt was holding a folder, which I assumed was mine. He asked me how I received my stripe. I told him about the CAP, US Air Force Base encampments and the Certificate of Proficiency. Apparently the program was still new enough or unknown enough that this was all news to the T.I.'s.

I (*correctly*) called the Sergeant by his rank "Technical Sergeant" as well as the Airman 1st and the Airman 3rd just Airman. The Sergeant said "I request that while in front of the troupes you address me and the other T.I.'s as SIR. I know that isn't required under AF Customs and Courtesies, but just in front of them I would appreciate it. Here you can call me Sarge if you like and them Airman."

"I think I can live with that Sarge! SIR!" and looked to the other T.I.'s and said "Sir's!" They all gave an uncustomary smile.

As we (*A/3c T.I. and I*) heading out of the barracks to rejoin the flight he said, "Think your a big man with that stripe don't you boy!"

"No bigger than you, Airman Smith, … SIR!" I responded in a voice only loud enough for him to hear.

In re-joining the flight we did some marching and for something I was required to answer him. I responded loud and clear "Yes, … **SIR!**" He smiled and he never bothered me from that moment on. We never developed much of a relationship and a few weeks later I think he was transferred to another flight or maybe he was awaiting Tech School and shipped out.

A couple days later the Sgt called me out of the ranks to his office and announced I would be the Flight secretary. He apologized that there were no empty quarters left in the barracks that I might have my own room. (*Note: I did know several other flights* (*barracks*) *appointed Flight Leaders and Flight Secretary but our T.I.'s hadn't.*) So I was acting as both the Flight Leader and Flight Secretary. That meant the Sergeant handed over all "administrative" duties (*his paperwork I assume*) for me to do. I made up the duty and KP rosters and, in what I considered a fair rotation, included myself to go to KP. He red lined me and said "You don't put yourself on anything unless I tell you to." As a result, I only pulled KP once in my 8 weeks of Basic Training. That happen only because the Sergeant needed to send every man in the barracks. (*I got Pots & Pans!*)

Remember the BIG earth shattering event that happen October 4th 1957? It was particularly devastating to the US military and to the Air Force in particular, It was like we were suddenly a second class country. I remember looking up in disgust as Sputnik whizzed across the cool crystal clear night sky in San Antonio, Texas. It was on everyone's tongue about how was it possible for the Russians to do something we couldn't do.

One cold 5am morning in November of 1957 it was huddling near zero degrees Fahrenheit. We were ordered to wear our big blue horse-blanket overcoats when we fell out. (We weren't issued fatigue jackets.) By noon that day the thermometer reached near 100 degrees. Almost a hundred degree shift in temperature. There we were, still marching around with a heavy wool coats on. Today they would call that cruel and unusual punishment. That night, most of us used our free (break) time standing in the shower.

Of course, a major event in the Basic Training saga is "shots day." We were in two lines, shirts off. As you proceeded down the line a Corpsman on both sides gave you his shots. Each Corpsman held three shots in his hand one syringe between each finger. (*One between the index finger and middle finger, one between the middle finger and the ring finger, and one between the ring finger and little finger.*) So you got the three needles at one punch and once the needles were in the Corpsman would squeeze his hand to deposit his juice from all three in one go. It was a very efficient method of getting six shots in a hurry. The big bruiser in front of me (*estimate about 6' 1" and 250 lbs*) took his shots and as he started to put his shirt on the Corpsman said, "Wait!" The Corpsman then proceeded to pull the needles back out of his arm. They detached from the syringe and the needles were stuck in him. Big bruiser takes a look at the Corpsman plucking the needles from him, goes white as a ghost and crumples to the floor. It takes four guys to carry him over to a nearby cot. The Corpsman totally uncaring, looks at me with a smile and said "Next!" I took a deep swallow and stepped forward. I was feeling lightheaded and thinking about that when the Corpsman said "Go, your done!" I swear I didn't feel it and didn't even realize I also received three shots on the other side by another Corpsman. Slick!

A couple days later we were marched to the Squadron HQ were we received the (*I think experimental*) "Flu Shot" via the air gun injection system. (*Needle-less*) That night I started running a fever and by morning I was sick as a dog. The T.I. told me to go to 'sick call' at the Base Hospital. I was pointed in the direction and left on my own to find it. There I am, near delirium wondering around the Base looking for the "sick-call" place. To this day I don't actually remember reaching the Hospital. The next thing I recall is waking up in a hospital bed to the announcement that I'd been in a three day coma. The Dr. said I had a severe adverse reaction to the Flu Shot. He gave me a prescription pad "order" and told me to carry it with me at all times that said I was never to take the flu shot again. That little piece of paper was as precious as gold throughout my stay in the Air Force. I don't know how many times they (*USAF*) would have Commander Calls and as you exited you were to receive a flu shot. I just presented my little slip of paper and got excused from receiving it. To this day I do not take the flu shot and amazingly, with all the various strains of the flu virus, I never get the flu. Maybe my system built up a whale of a bunch of antibodies against those little buggers.

I was fortunate to be released from the Hospital in time that I wasn't assigned to another Flight because I missed five days of training. I think if you miss six or more days you were washed back to another flight. The Sergeant jokingly accused me of flaking off but there was a stack of paperwork waiting for me to catchup. The A/1c T.I. grumbled that he had to do my work while I "rested."

At the Green Monster we were 'counseled' about our career options based on the scores from the tests we had taken. I recall one of the guys in the barracks telling me he didn't care what he got, but definitely did not want to be a radio operator stating, "My brother is a ham operator and all the time I listened to dit- dit- daha- daha- daha, to the wee hours of the morning. That would drive me nuts!" On one of our test days we were given a radio Morse code recognition test. They gave us a newfangled answer sheet that was electronically scored. They started off with daha-dit and told us to use our #2 pencil and block in the letter 'A'. Then they did dit-daha and told to fill in the letter 'B' following that they did dit-dit for 'C' and daha-daha for 'D'. Then they told us to see how many we could distinguish, adding that we should leave it blank if we were not sure what it was, in-other-words don't just guess. Well my friend certainly doesn't want to be a radio operator so he lays his pencil down and leaves the rest of his test sheet blank. Days later when we go back to the Green Monster he is told he will be a Radio operator and would be sent directly to Tech Code school. How is that possible? Because he got 100% on his code test. The score was based on number right to number attempted and because he enter on his sheet the A-B-C-D he attempted 4 and got 4 right – 100%. A test scoring machine scored the answer sheet and this precursor of a computer can't lie (*or think*).

For me it was a different story. In my councilor session the Sergeant told me I had choices, based on my scores. I could be a Water Purification Specialist, (*I think that is someone that digs latrines*) or a Draftsman, or a Artist. (*Interesting that the tests they give did pick up on my art background but I don't quite understand the shit strainer one.*) I explained to the Sergeant I wanted to be a Photographer. "Can't!" he replied, "The Photo Tech School is closed. You have to put the three I offered in the order of your preference." Well, I at least learned that the Air Force never gives you your first choice so I said "Water Purification Specialist, Artist, Draftsman, in that order.

Back at the barracks I was really bummed out when I heard one of the guys mention he was going to be a photographer. "How in the hell did you get that?" I questioned. He said he worked in a photo processing place before joining and took the bypass specialist test in photography. Seems if you take the test and pass it you don't go to Tech School, you go directly to your duty assignment. I was really pissed off that I didn't know about this avenue and when I returned to the Green Monster for my so called final interview the Sergeant proudly announced that I was going to be an Artist and said he would have orders cut for me to go to Art Tech School. I asked him if I could take the bypass specialist test for Photographer. He looked at me like I just shoved a knife in his back. "Where did you hear about that?" he said. I told him one of the guys in my barracks and that I had a hell of a lot more experience than he did. The Sergeant said "You can't pass it, it is very technical and uses Air Force nomenclature." I figured if the guy in the barracks that just processed film could pass it so could I, so I ask again if I could take the Bypass Specialist test. He relented saying, "You can take it, you won't pass it and you will be an Artist, but I will schedule you for the test."

Test day arrives! I was pumped and ready. Much to my dismay the first question starts off "When using Armed Forces Developer #1 the effect on the film is:" What? I'll leave that one blank. Second question, "When using a C-6 camera" another "The C-1 camera is best for..." Oh shit, I thought, I'm in deep trouble here, ... I have no clue what these are. Fortunately as I progressed though the test, leaving most of it blank I came across references where the C-6 was a 4x5 format camera. So, based on my experience, I answered all the questions assuming a C-6 camera was a graphic press camera. Same thing about a C-1 being a 35mm range finder camera and later Armed Forces Developer #1 was a fine grain developer so I acted like it must be D-76 film developer. I kept finding references to what I was familiar with and substituting. I thank my lucky stars to have been so well grounded in such a wide variety of areas by George Wisler. It was his great tutelage that got me through the test.

Back to the Green Monster to get the results. The Sergeant recognizes me and pulls out my file. He reads the results and looks up at me and said, "You cheated. I don't know how you cheated, but you must have cheated. Of the 128 questions on the test you got a 123 correct."

"Does that mean I passed?" I asked.

"Well, ... yeah, damn near aced it!" He sighed, "Looks like you are going to be a Photographer. You will get your orders a couple days before graduation as to the base you will be assigned."

"As a photographer? No school?" I asked.

"Yes, you will be assigned as a 3 level 2 3 2 3 0 still photographer, same as if you completed Photo Technical School." Poor guy, he really looked like I ruined his day, but inside I was screaming for joy. I could hardly wait to find out where I would be assigned.

The day the orders came was very exciting. The fella that told me about the Bypass Specialist Test was going to a Aerial Recon Squadron at Shaw AFB where he would be processing and printing aerial film. I sure didn't want to do that for my Air Force career. I got assigned to the Base Photo Lab, 78th ADC (*Air Defense Command*) Wing at Hamilton AFB, at Navato/San Rafael, California, (*which I found out later was the "Country Club of the Air Force"*). Base Photo Labs were the best assignments as it meant you shot pictures. I was in heaven!

Hamilton AFB

After graduation from Basic Training I took a short leave at home. I decided to go to California on a train called "The City of San Francisco" out of Chicago. It was necessary for my dad to take me to Bellefontaine, Ohio first to catch a train that went to the station in Chicago. What an adventure. It was the first time I had been on a train. There I was an 18 year old, now a full fledged member of the Armed Forces, crossing the country on my own, heading off to my first Base. I was screaming inside with excitement.

I arrived at Hamilton AFB in mid December 1957. After processing in and meeting my new Squadron First Sergeant, Master Sergeant Obey. He asked if I objected to sharing a room with a "colored man." I was actually shocked and taken back by the question. Back in the CAP two of my best friends Lester Swanson (*My First Sergeant*) and Tony Palmer (*a Flight Leader*) were blacks and came to my house quite often. As the Cadet Commander I would have Commanders Call (*an excuse for a party*) at my house about every time I babysit my Sister. I never considered Lester or Tony any different than the other guys (*and gals*) in the Squadron. In fact, the only time their race ever came up was one time Mom said to me, "Are you having colored boys coming to the house when you babysit?" I told her yes, that they were part of my Cadet Squadron.

She said "You know, … it looks funny to the neighbors to have *"them folks"* coming to the house." I was shocked and told her, "Mom, … if Lester and Tony are not welcome in this house neither am I." She apologized and never brought up the subject again. I guess Mom and Dad were brought up in an environment that folks in that era had a different take on race. In fact, my dear Aunt Blanch (*Mom's Sister*) was, despite her very religious lifestyle, also very racist. I once asked her, "BG (*Blanch Grady was her name and my Sister was the one that named her BG by initials*) what will you do if you get to Heaven and find Saint Peter at the Golden Gate is a black man?" She thought a minute and said, "I'll say Praise the Lord(*N word*), … let me in."

So, obviously I didn't think there was a thing wrong with sharing a room with a "colored man." Well, the fellows name was Theodore (*Ted*) R. Curry and he was one of the finest and most memorable men I ever met. He was an A/1c, a photographer in the Photo Lab. I think Ted was about 31 or 32 years old, thin and six foot tall. He had a young "Morgan

Freeman" face and expressions to go with any occasion. In fact, Ted 'looked' younger than me. He had the only car among the single members of the Photo Lab, so whenever we wanted to party in San Francisco we counted on Ted to get us there (*and back*). But I get ahead of myself.

Being the newbie in the Photo Lab they were anxious to put me to work ASAP by pulling "Alert." (*Alert Photographer – meant being available to photograph anything the Air Force needed pictures of. In most cases it was auto-accidents, breaking and entering photo evidence, occasionally some after hours or weekend activity. On rare occasions, thank heavens, was it something messy like a murder or a suicide or worse, a plane crash. The point was you needed to be ready and available at a moments notice if you were on Alert Duty.*) I think I arrived to the Base on a Wednesday and reported to the Base Photo Lab on Thursday. After the NCOIC (*Non-Commissioned Officer In Charge (M/Sgt Mosby)*) check me out to see if I knew HOW to take a picture, load 4x5 film holders, compute an exposure both by using a light meter or using a flash bulbs in the dark. I passed his muster and he decided I "squeaked by" as a photographer. He promptly put me on Alert starting Friday night and for the rest of the weekend. He showed me the "Alert Room," which was a small room in the lab with a desk, a phone, a cot, couch, an easy chair w/reading lamp and a refrigerator. "No alcoholic beverages." he warned. He gave me the "Alert Keys" consisting of the Photo Lab's front door key and keys to the Camera equipment and photo supplies room. He said I was permitted to go to the Chow Hall, Barracks (*for showering/change clothes – but not sleeping*), PX, Concession Ice Cream Stand, and Base Movie Theater, so long as I called the Air Police. He said "Tell them where you're at, were you're going to be, and route you're taking, just in case they need to pick you up." As an Alert Photographer you received a special chow pass, a card that allowed you go to "chow" at anytime, night or day. You could also go to the Base movie free, because, ... as it happened a few times to me, a small sign would appear along the bottom of the screen that said "Alert Photographer report to lobby." and you didn't see the rest of the movie. (*No big deal. A first run movie only cost 25 cents and popcorn or coke was only a dime!*)

Friday evening, I was alone. I went to chow with the other guys in the Photo Lab and they all heading out to San Francisco, so I walked back to the lab. You can't imagine my excitement. Me, Jim Voris, Official USAF Photographer, standing Alert. I was ready, ... for anything, … I thought. Friday night clicks by, I can hardly sleep and an empty Photo Lab makes a lot of weird sounds at night. It was about 11pm when the NCOIC came into the lab. I was still awake and came out to see who it was that came in. He was probably just there making sure that I was there and he said to check to see if I was alright or had any questions. He seemed satisfied everything was OK and left. It was an uneventful night. No calls – nothing. I was very disappointed. Saturday morning I walked to chow, and returned straight to the lab. I checked-out the camera assortment in the Equipment room. Nothing new and a lot needing repair. But I familiarize myself with what's there, what works and what doesn't. Lunch at the Chow Hall, I stop by the PX (*Post Exchange*) on the way back to the Photo Lab to pick up some personal items and some Cokes to put in the refrigerator. I am beginning to think that being an Air Force Photographer is kinda boring and wondering if maybe being a "Water Purification Specialist" wouldn't have been so bad. I was getting ready to go to the Chow Hall for supper when the phone rang. I was startled by it, as this was the first time it rung since I came on duty.

"This is the Air Police, we have a plane down and the Flying Safety officer is heading to the Photo Lab right now to pick up the Alert Photographer. Is he there and ready to go?"

With a lump in my throat I responded, "Yes, I am the Alert Photographer and will be standing out front for pick-up!" I got a "Roger that!" and hung up. I grabbed my Camera case and flashbulb bag and ran out the door. The Flying Safety Officer was at the lab within seconds of my coming outside and I dropped my stuff in the back seat and jumped into the jeep he was driving. He was a Captain and I was thinking, maybe I should have saluted as I approached the jeep, but the subject never came up. He said that a C-45 had gone down shortly after take off and was just a short distance off base in the hills of San Rafael. We didn't speak as we rushed to the site of the crash. We ended up near the top of a mountain (*they call it a hill but to me it was a mountain*) and the aircraft had flat pancaked into the ground. It must have been going awful slow when it hit because the plane appeared to be fairly intact. It was getting late into dusk hours and AF vehicles surround the craft putting on their headlights to illuminate the crash site. The FSO (*Flying Safety Officer*) said that he needed a picture of the instrument panel so we needed to enter the craft. It had been "foamed down" and it was obvious there had not been a fire. When we stepped inside there was aviation gas standing a inch or so deep on the floor in places as the full fuel cells ruptured on impact but fortunately not exploded. The gas fumes took our breath away as we made our way to the front of the aircraft. At the Cockpit the windshield was all cracked up but in place. The pilot and co-pilot were both dead and still in their seats, but the seats were forced up against the instrument panel. The FSO carefully pulled the bodies back from the instrument panel as best he could and said "Can you get a picture of the full panel?" I already put the wide angle lens on, dropped the bed on the camera and reset the rangefinder to match the wide angle lens. Although it was getting very dark, especially inside the plane, I felt I could get the shot. To focus, the 4x5 graphic camera had a rangefinder on the side so if you connected a cord from the flash tube it would power small red lights inside the range finer projecting two beams. If you could bring the two dots together it meant it was in focus. Earlier that day I discovered a special cord back at the Photo Lab equipment room. I recognized what it was from my days with George Wisler. I put it in my flash bulb bag just for such an occasion. I was ready for my shot. Set my exposure for the required flash, which was a #22 flash bulb. (*the same size in dimensions of a 100 watt light bulb*) I recall the FSO looking at me as I went about diligently preparing for my first exposure. **POP** went the flash and the FSO jumped. He said, "Okay we need some shots outside." I said, "Wait sir, I always shoot a backup shot and **POP** another of the panel from a slightly different prospective. "Okay, okay that's enough, lets get outside." I recall vaguely putting the expended flash bulbs in my bag but not positive. A #22 is very hot and it takes a few seconds for it to cool down after it flashes so I would have to wait that long just to change the bulb for the second shot. Anyway, we exited the wreckage and got my other shots.

As we were heading back to base I was ecstatic with my first official Air Force job under my belt. I felt that now I really was a AF photographer.

As we pulled up to the photo lab to drop me off the FSO said "Good job Airman. I will say you are certainly one of the bravest photographers I have ever been with."

"How's that Sir?" While I appreciated the compliment, I did not have a clue what he meant about me being brave.

"Welllll, … you knew that, ..." he said clearing his throat, "the heat of the flash bulb could set off the gas fumes and we would have been blown sky high. I was really amazed when you calmly went about doing the second shot in there."

I know I must have turned as white as a ghost and about to wet myself as I said, "No, Sir. You would be the brave one. I didn't know what could happen, … you did!"

I am sure as the FSO tells the same story he starts it off with, "I was with this idiot photographer once that..."

I often wondered if safety in an explosive environment was a subject I missed by not going to Photo Tech School. The headlines could have easily read A/3c Jim Voris, exploded on his very first "official" photo exposure as an USAF photographer. A real "flash in the pan, that boy!"

First Job-First Mistake

Monday morning I had my shots processed and printed one set and proudly presented them to the Lab Chief (*Master Sgt Mosebe*). I was immediately chewed out. Because in order for me to process the film it was necessary to be in total darkness. If as Alert Photographer I was needed "right now" I would have NOT been available because I was processing film. The other alternative was if I opened the door to exit I would have lost the film (*and the mission pictures*) or it would be necessary to leave the film in chemicals not knowing how long I would be gone which would again destroy or at least damage the film. There again compromising the mission. I was getting an education. I again did not have the experience or know all the rules. After getting properly dress down I was told I had done an excellent job on the shots. He then said that I had the next three days off. I thought I was being punished but the Lab Chief explained that I was getting off because I pulled three Alerts in a row. (*You got one day off for every day you pulled Alert*) What in the world was I going to do with three days off? I spent Monday morning exploring the base and getting my bearings. I met the photo lab guys at noon in the chow hall and wandered around some more until supper. I met the guys again and Ted (*my room mate*) offered to take me to town and get a beer. (*Note at the time you could drink 3.2 beer in Ohio at 18 years old but in California you must be 21, even for 3.2 beer – if you could find it.*) I told him I was underage and he said he knew a bar that wasn't picky – so we went. It was a great time and I vaguely remember Ted dropping me in my sack that night, stoned. To this day I get drunker on beer than the hard stuff.

Tuesday I went into the Photo Lab and worked anyway, printing as it turned out, umpteen copies of my shots of the Plane Crash for the Crash Investigation inquiry board. One of the photographers went Monday to shoot the pilot's and co-pilot's autopsy. Several of the guys congratulated me on the great job I did on the pictures and all were good exposures. Sgt Mosebe reminded me I didn't have to be there but I explained I didn't have anything else I needed to do and this was what I liked to do. I apologized again for processing the film and realized why it was wrong to do so.

He said "No harm done this time and as it worked out, the OIC (*Officer in Charge*) - Captain King, took your photos to an early meeting on Monday and the Lab received praise for the quick work. He said the FSO commented on the courage of the photographer." Sergeant Mosebe looked knowingly at me, winked and said, "You are a very lucky young man." I felt pale and replied "Yes Sir! But that won't happen again, … Sir."

Well, maybe not that exact same thing, but then I have a LOT of learning to do!

Christmas 1957

I offered to be the Alert Photographer over the entire Christmas/New Years days off. Everyone was thrilled to have the newbie take the duty. Everyone was talking about going places for Christmas and even the single guys had girlfriends they wanted to be with. My girlfriend, Melanie, was way back in Ohio and still in High School. There was nothing for me to do, so I was happy to take the full duty. Sgt Mosebe winked at me saying, "Don't blow yourself up while we're gone! If you need anything or help, just call me and I'll have someone here to help you."

So, I became the Alert Photographer on Monday evening, December 23rd 1957 and would be on duty until the morning of Thursday, January 2nd 1958. Ten days running, 24 hours of on call duty. I remember there was only one job during that whole time period. It was a seven car pileup outside the Main gate on highway 101, that involved a military truck somewhere in the lineup. While I was shooting pictures, some woman passing the mess slammed on her brakes to see what was going on and, **BAMM**, <u>crash</u>, *tinkle*, **crunch**, squeal, ***thud***, <u>boom</u>, etc, ect. There was another larger, twelve-car pileup next to the one we were covering. (*If it involves a government vehicle we shot pictures of it for the Air Police -that second pileup* *didn't - so we weren't involved.*) I do recall though, the CHP's (*California Highway Patrol*) officer taking off his hat and throwing it on the ground as he was cussing. Apparently they were short handed for the holiday schedule too, and he was going to have to handle all the accident reports alone.

The first few days were so quiet I think half the base went home for the Christmas Holidays. I borrowed a reel to reel tape deck (*from Ted I think*) and played around talking on it to myself. I would play like I was a radio announcer and interview people on the street, playing all the parts, adding sound effects occasionally (*crashes, sirens, that sort of thing. I would have long one sided conversations with Melanie (my girlfriend in Ohio who ultimately became my dear wife and the mother of my great kids – but more on that later.*) I sent these tapes to her. I do recall they were very funny, but maybe in a disturbed way. I was bored to tears and this was my only outlet.

A day or two after Christmas several of the Photo Lab guys came in and we just talked and told jokes. Ted knew I was going stir crazy and he was a welcome sight. I played some of my tapes and then everyone wanted in on it. For a while I 'off the cuff' unrehearsed "street interviews" that were deliriously funny. Somewhere in our "stuff" are the old tapes but I am sure now the oxide has deteriorated and they are unrecoverable (*and likely not in the least bit humorous. Scary maybe, but probably not as funny as I thought they were! Better to let the memory be whatever it wants to be.*)

Ted Curry was the mother of the group and looked after all of us. (*Over the ensuing years I have attempted a number of time to find Ted but no success.*) He dropped in to the Photo Lab several times during my Christmas/New Years Alert marathon just to chat and make sure I was okay. S/Sgt Edwards came by, as well as M/Sgt Mosebe, T/Sgt Merrill Myers, S/Sgt Bobby (*forget her last name*). What a really great bunch to work with and for. I don't recall Captain King or Lt Riker stopping by but everyone else did. I felt I become a full fledged member of the team and it was smart of me to volunteer.

One of the other things I could do was "play" in the darkroom printing as this didn't involve any commitment that could damage a mission. We were allowed to use a certain percentage of the supplies for "training purposes" so I was experimenting with darkroom imagery. I previously created a time exposure of a swinging light in a dark room that gave a interesting geometric pattern. I coupled that with flicks of hypo onto exposed paper and the processed image looked like my pattern floating in outer-space. I called it "Creation in Space" I later submitted it in an Air Force photo contest and it won first place in a "creative image" category. I got a three day pass out of it and some recognition.

In January we added A/2c Larry Ryberg, a handsome, mountain of a man, at 6' 3" about 280 pounds of rock hard muscle. His official job title was "draftsman" (*Funny, if I had become a draftsman I might have ended up in a Base Photo Lab anyway*) but in truth, he actually was assigned to the base as a football player. Larry spent half of everyday, working out at the base gym. During football season, we hardly saw him - unless it was an "on base" game. Then of course we all showed up. If we weren't there assigned to photograph it, we were there to cheer for Larry and the Base Team. But, his official job as "draftsman" consisted of him lettering negatives. Larry was married to the most adorable little wife. Their house was off base in San Rafael. Larry loved to party and there were many parties at his house. We would also run over to Stinson Beach, north of the Golden Gate Bridge on the coast. The first time I saw the ocean I was awestruck. I was a "flat lander" - raised in Ohio and only seen the ocean once before in my life. I was about 7 years old and Dad was getting out of the service after the war. Mom's sister and her sisters husband (*Blanch and Hayden Grady*) drove us "out west" to be with Dad who was in the Navy. He still had a few months to go before being mustered out. (*It was the end of WWII*) We were staying in military dependent housing off base and I was in 1st grade at John Muir Elementary School a few blocks from our quarters. Because of the huge number of kids the school was on half day schedule. We went to school at 9 and got out at 11:30. During that (*rigorous and grueling*) 2 ½ hours (*of education?*) we managed to get in 6 recesses. (*As you can guess my California educational foundation … sucked*). Anyway, that is the reason we were in California and why as a 7 year old I came to see the ocean. I suppose it was a Sunday and we took the bus to the beach. (*Not taking any swim suits – don't think Mom or I even owned one.*) I recall Mom taking my shoes off and we walked on the beach through the sand. I saw a wave wash up really far and ran to get my feet in the water and then running with it as it receded. Dad is shouting for me to stop. Being the obedient son, I did, in fact I froze. Just then another wave came crashing in, hit me full body and I went ass end over teacup. Fully clothed, I was dragged through the water/sand mixture like being in a tumble clothes washer. Dad ran in and grabbed me lifting me up out of the water but the next waves undertow knocked him off balance and plop! Dad ends up in the drink. Did I mention that Dad was in his navy whites and that his service cap fell off in the mayhem and was on its way to somewhere in the far east? I could also mention that getting a couple swats across the fanny when your wearing wet, sand filled clothes stings a lot. Well, the bus ride back home was not like the other people's ride. They were all laughing and talking about their beautiful day at the beach. Dad and I had to stand and walk funny with that sand in our shorts. For some reason we didn't go to the beach again, so I only seen the ocean once. For me the ocean was a traumatic event.

So my first time (*as an adult*) seeing the ocean was both terrifying and awe inspiring. Anyone that has ever been to the beach around San Francisco know how cold the sea water is. In the mid 50's on a good day. My first experience of entering the water was on one of our beach party outings. I recall standing at the waters edge and watched the waves crashing in. I stood for the longest time mustering the courage to just run in. (*Like the other guys in the Photo Lab.*) A wave came farther up and though it was only slightly deeper than my ankles the pull of the water and undertow knocked me down and rolled me closer to the wave break line. Before I knew it another wave hit me and rolled me up on the beach. I was sputtering and laughing at the same time. I was having a flash back to Dad doing the same thing twelve years before in San Diego. I eventually went in and did all the things everyone else was doing. (*Last time I was in San Francisco along the beach I notice everyone in the water was wearing diver skins. Woocies!*)

A few months passed and new folks began arriving at the Photo Lab. A/3c Rubin Sanchez (*a Camera repairman*) and A/3c Johnny Brunner, A/3c Glenda Tate (*WAF*) and A/3c "Spinny" Spinyortus (*WAF*) Except for Rubin, all the others were photographers. All, I might add, graduates from the newly reopened Photo Tech School that I didn't go to.

More Lessons

How Bright I Am!

One night while on Alert, I received a call from the Base Public Relations office. They stated I was needed at the Flight Line in forty-five minutes, dress in my Class "A" Blues. It seems a 3 star General was making a surprise visit and despite the hour (*it would be nearly 10:00pm by the time he arrived.*) full military honors would still be given. (*Meaning a band and the Base Commander would be there greeting him.*) Well, ... I made it and my dress blues were jammed pack with good old #22 flash bulbs. As the plane approached the ramp all of a sudden I lit up. All the flashbulbs that were in my pockets ignited simultaneously. (*Did I mention before about how frigging hot they are when they ignite?*) As the aircraft rolled to a stop I was literally on the ground rolling to smother the smoking uniform. My legs were burned from the ones in my pockets and my thighs were roasted from the ones in my blouse jacket. The band barely started playing when I lit up. The Base Commander and 3 star General came over to me on the ground.

"What happen here?" the 3 star asked.

"Some dumb son-of-a-bitch forgot to turn off the radar." I said, in not a moderate tone, then I saw who ask!

"Sorry son, I was the dumb son-of-a-bitch. I was the AC (*Aircraft Commander/Pilot*) and you're right. I forgot to turn off the radar." I heard him say to the Base Commander, "Use my staff car and rush this man to the hospital."

One of the Honor Guard told me later, "Man when those bulbs went off I swear I could see clean through you, ... like an x-ray."

At the hospital they treated me for minor burns on my legs and hips with big burn bandages. Sgt Mosebe had been notified and was at the hospital not very long after I arrived. While he was glad to see I was okay, admonished me for having the flashbulbs in my pockets and not in the bulb bag where they were suppose to be. I explained that I was trying to look "dressed" and that the rag-tagged canvas bag (*like an old WWII knapsack*) looked totally out of place. I also tried to point out that it got in the way when you were shooting. You either set it down or have the cumbersome bag on your arm which hindered shooting good candid shots. While he generally agreed, he reminded me that the bag was a safety measure and the incident only proved why we needed to keep the bulbs away from contact with our body. I was hardly in a position to disagree with the wisdom of that rule. I told him I chalked up another learning experience, short of blowing myself up. I was immediately released back to duty but Sgt Mosebe already pulled in another photographer to take over "Alert" that night. He said I could have the next day off but I decided to work anyway. (*I knew I would get light duty at the Photo Lab. If I couldn't be out shooting, I would want to be printing pictures in the Air Conditioned darkroom. It's what I loved to do.*)

The next day, as expected I am in the darkroom printing pictures when over the the intercom comes, "Airman Voris report to the office." Utt

Ohh, one always expects the worse when one is "called to the office." I wondered what I had done that I was going to get chewed out for. (*Note: Despite being raised Baptist, I had the Catholic mentality that I was guilty of everything!*) Seems the 3 Star General came in to the lab to see **me**. I was told later that upon entering the Lab he said, "Is that Airman I fried last night on duty today?" As soon as I saw him in the office (*Actually, what I SAW was three STARS flashing*) I figured I was in really deep doo-doo, kem-che – whatever, over calling him a stupid son-of-a-bitch for leaving the Radar on. (*I wondered where the Air Police were to haul me off to the dungeon. Do they give you a cigarette before they put the blindfold on you at the stake and shoot you. These were the things flashing through my mind!*) I snapped to attention and saluted, and immediately apologized for my outburst.

He quickly countered, "No, no you were right. I was a stupid son-of-a-bitch. It was my responsibility to shut the radar off. But tell me, instead of getting rid of all the dumb SOB's in the Air Force what could we do to prevent this from happening in the future?

In the corner of my eye I saw Sgt Mosebe start to say something (*probable to explain to the General about my lack of safety and inexperience.*) when I immediately popped in and said "Well Sir, if we had electronic flash units for use in flight line applications and explosive environments (*I had to add that!*) it couldn't happen. I glanced to Capt King and Sgt Mosebe and they had a shocked look on their face. The lab put in for two electronic flash units but the budget was cut so we didn't get them.

The General immediately said "Tell me the exact name and nomenclature of what you need." The next day two Heiland Professional Strobe units were dropped off to the Photo Lab with a note attached. "I'll try to get a little smarter, but in the meantime let's not fry anymore Airman." Signed General (*Sorry, I don't remember his name*). He had gone downtown San Francisco (*or more likely sent his Aide*) and purchased the two units from a professional photography supply house, out of his own pocket (*or budget?*).

The Gipper has taken one for the boys and was now the hero.*(Well at least for a little while.)*

4th Air Force

Too Much of a Good Thing

One tenant organization housed at Hamilton AF Base was 4th Air Force Headquarters, Commanded by a one star General, Brigadier Gen Sory Smith. Colonel Celears was our 78th Wing Base Commander who was a Full Bird Colonel, but that is one rank lower than a Brigadier General. 4th AF had their own Public Relation office run by two Master Sergeant's that were great guys, but they didn't have a photographer assigned to their office. (*Sorry I do not recall their names at this writing.*) After I happen to shoot a couple assignment with them they seemed to like my work and in particular seemed to take a personal liking to me. They introduced me to General Smith and Jim Voris soon became 4th Air Force's Official Photographer. I was requested by name and got to go on some really choice TDY's (*Temporary Duty Assignments*) like to Las Vegas, Nevada to the 4th AF Reunion. There I got to shoot famous people like General Jimmy Doolittle, movie stars (*like Jimmy Stewart*) and starlets. I even got a dance with Ronda Fleming (*a really beautiful woman*). Harold's Club gave us complimentary rooms and there was $20 in gambling chips on the bed each night (*incentive to gamble of course*) but I used mine mostly for food (*and drinks*). In addition when you are on TDY you get money for lodging and food to boot so it was a money making deal for this young airman. Soon I started getting letters of Commendation from General Smith. Because they were a tenant organization it had to go all the way to ADC HQ, to the Wing HQ. to the Squadron Commander to be read and awarded at the next appropriate Commanders Call in front of the whole squadron. The first one, even the first two, the Lab Officer Captain King and Lt Richart thought was good for the lab but when at a Commanders call the Commander was required to read three of the "Letters of Commendation" along with endorsements from ADC and the Wing HQ. for one Airman James L. Voris and his "exemplary photography" it became more than the office (*or squadron*) could bear. I was ordered not to go on any more 4th Air Force photo assignments. I begged the General to stop sending the letters but he said it looked good in my file and just ignored my plea. The Sergeant from 4th AF would call the Lab for a photo shoot and request me and they would say I was on another assignment. They would respond that they would wait until I came back or was available. Then it got to the point the Generals office would call and request me by name, what could they do. The General did finally agree to stop sending letters but there were two still in the system. The Photo Lab Lt was pissed at me. He thought I was trying to be some kind of show off - grand-stander. It really was the farthest thing from my mind and I avoided every job I could with 4th AF. But then, one fateful Saturday the Sergeant at 4th AF begged me to shoot a movie for them of a simulated rescue. It was way off base up in the hills it was going to be fun, fun, fun they insisted, so I relented and agreed to do it. The scenario of the shots were a boy scout was suppose to be injured. A 4th AF rescue helicopter comes in, drops a smoke marker to indicate where he is and a ground rescue units saves the boy. A one hour shooting schedule at most. I agreed but said I absolutely positively needed to be back on base at 8:00pm to shoot a job at the Officers Club for the Officers Wives Club. They guaranteed we would be back in "plenty of time with hours to spare."

Movies are not generally shot in sequence that you see them. Sometimes the end is shot in the middle the middle at the beginning the beginning at the end of the shoot, like that. In our case the guys rescuing the boy scout were there before the chopper arrived so we shot the sequences of them wrapping up the boy scouts leg and arm and getting ready for transport. As the chopper arrived he dropped his smoke marker to indicate the alleged location where the ground rescuers were to come. Of all the places the marker should hit – dead center on a rock – and it exploded into a fire ball. (*it is not suppose to do that!*) Well, California is noted for it's wild-fires. All of a sudden here was this dry, dry, grass wildfire being fanned by this chopper sitting directly overhead. We're all screaming trying to wave off the chopper but it seems he had no idea what we are attempting to say until it's too late and he saw large flames raising. He then veers off and gets the hell out of there. I am standing on the crest of the hill waving down at the sheriff of Marin County (*who was suppose to be in part of the movie*) who waves back until he sees a lot of smoke raise up and I see him run for his radio. I was using my AF Uniform coat to beat out grass flames until the fire fighters got there. The poor boy scout (*actor*) had to hobble and jump to keep out of the flames as he was all bandaged up and had a hell of a time trying to get out of his bandages.

It was almost 8:30 that evening when I finally got back to the base. I was filthy. The 4th AF guys apologetically dropped me at my barracks. I ran in, took a quick shower, slipped into a new uniform, and sprinted to the photo lab to grab my equipment for the assignment. **BAM!** There standing at the door was Lt Richart with an awful evil look on his face like, ... "*I got you sucker.*" I froze and just stood there looking as guilty as a kid caught with his hand in the cookie jar. I knew I was had.

He said with a calm gotcha voice, “I sent the Alert photographer to cover your job and I am standing by for the Alert just in case. But before I nail your hide to the wall I would **love** to hear your **'excuse'** for missing your mission.” He really punched the word ***excuse***.

I swallowed hard and said, “I, … I, had to fight a forest fire sir.” Now in California they can stop you on the highway and press an able-bodied man into service to fight a forest fire. Now I admit, I didn't mention that it was caused by 4th Air Force and that I was there on a 4th AF mission, but, ... then he didn't ask why I was there either.

It worked. The evil grin drained from his face and he stammered. “Ohhh, ... Ohh, … well, … okay, … then, ahh, ...” He paused a moment then said before making a hasty retreat, “You stand by here until the Alert Photographer returns.”

Shine the Walls

Pay Ahead

A few weeks later Lt Rikert called me up to the office and started railing on me about something he said I did. (*Actually I hadn't. One of the other guys in the lab did, I knew who did, but I just kept my mouth shut.*) He concluded his outrage with, "... and for the next 30 days every night from 6 pm to 9 pm you will be down here in this photo lab scrubbing it down with a tooth brush. Do you understand? And, I will be checking on you to make sure your are working every minute. Got it?"

"Yes Sir!" I respond very calmly. (*I can't say I looked forward to this, but it really wasn't that bad. After all, I wasn't like the other guys in the lab. They had a "life" outside the lab, but for me it was something to do. It actually wasn't a tooth brush, a bristle hand brush was issued to me.*)

The Photo Lab had glazed tile walls and floors. I was making a visible difference. The place was beginning to sparkle like a gem. But, true to his word, Lt Rikert would often be there or drop in at exactly 6 pm to make sure I was there and began work "on time." He often dropped in at exactly 9 pm to make sure I was still working up to the appointed minute. In fact, one time I had a small section left of a wall yet to finish and it was shortly after 9. Probably about 9:10. I was up on my ladder scrubbing away and Lt Rikert came in and watched me a few seconds and then said, "It's after nine, you can quit!"

"Yes Sir, I know. I just want to finish this little spot here, then this room will be done." He didn't say anything else, he just quietly left.

When my 30 days were up he called me up to the office and said, "Well, … I will have to hand it to you Airman Voris, you took your punishment like a man. As far as I'm concerned the matter is closed."

"Sir, I would like to tell you now that I didn't do what you accused me of." I said with relish.

He looked at me amazed, "What? Why didn't you tell me, why didn't you say something then?"

"Sir, I have been led to believe in the Air Force we are suppose to do as we are told FIRST and, if time and circumstance permit, complain later.. I did as I was told, … Sir, … now I am complaining."

He flushed in embarrassment and said, "I am sorry I didn't at least ask you if you did it, I just assumed. Well, there is nothing I can do to undo the last 30 days, but say that I am sorry and I owe you a big one."

Thereafter everyone's little mistakes that might get them in "trouble" with the Lt, I would immediately jump in and say "I'm sorry Lt Richart, I did that!" He would mumble and say something about I already spent my time in hell and let the issue drop.

Hamilton Photographers (and wives) 30th reunion 1958-88

(Sidebar note: In 1988 a bunch of us 'ol Hamilton photographers had a 30th year reunion in San Francisco and went out to Hamilton. The Base had been decommissioned and much of it demolished but the photo lab building was still there. As we peeked in the windows everyone commented on how shiny and polished the walls still looked!)

One evening when I was walking back to the Photo Lab from the barracks after a shower and uniform change, I observed a beautiful German Sheppard loping along down the center of the street. I whistled, calling to him and he immediately came over to me. I could see that he had a Air Police collar on him, so I had to assume he had escaped from his normal assigned area. He was as friendly as a puppy and wanted to be petted and talked to, which I was eager to supply. I knelt down and scratched behind his ears and under his chin which he seemed to enjoy. After a few minutes I decided I better notify someone as to his whereabouts. There was a phone booth about half a block away so I instructed him to follow me, which he obediently complied. There, I called the Air Police and asked if they were missing a guard dog. They immediately responded with "Yes!" and wanted to know where I had last seen him. I told them I had him with me outside the phone booth giving a location. They said to carefully lock myself inside the booth as the dog was "very dangerous" and they would be at my location ASAP. I felt that was ridiculous, so I got out of the phone booth, told the dog to get in, and slowly closed the door leaving a small crack opening. I talked softly to the dog and petted him through the crack. He was alright, perfectly calm, … that is until the Air Police trucks starting coming with sirens and lights flashing. Then he went wild. I had betrayed him. I was holding the door shut with my full weight when they pulled up. They shot him with a tranquilizer gun to calm him down and I was crying. Why was this beautiful animal being treated so harshly was beyond me. He was not cut out to be a guard dog was my thinking, he just wanted to be loved. I was very upset, but I didn't know what else I could have done. The Sgt in charge of the detail thanked me for my "actions" and wanted to know if I would consider cross training into K-9 corps. I said angerly, "Not on your life!" I still get teary eyed thinking about the event and often wonder about how that dog eventually ended up.

On a lighter note, one late night, about 2:30am, I came back to the barracks from being in San Francisco (*partying of course*) and I was very … happy. What is the first thing you do when you "get home" after a lot of ... happiness? You go to the "potty!" Well I stagger in to the latrine and as I am standing at the urinal I am aware that there is someone else in the latrine. To my back is two rows of toilets. The military didn't believe in privacy in 1958 and there were 7 toilets on one side of the wall and 7 on the other. Sitting in left side middle toilet was a woman. She waved at me!

I quickly recovered my family hardware and shoved it back in my pants (*I am not to sure I was finished*) as I stared at the wall in front of me.

Once all tucked in and zipped up, I rushed back outside and stood there looking at the barracks number going over and over it in my mind to make sure it was the correct barracks. (*An alcohol clouded mind sometimes has to check and re-check the facts.*) Once fully convinced and now sober from the adrenalin shock, out the barracks door comes the young lady and said to me as she passes, "Damn fine latrine you have there!" I immediately rush up to the room and wake Ted to tell him there had been a woman in our latrine. "Ahh, your drunk and seeing thing Voris, go to bed!" I told other guys in the barracks too but nobody believed me! I never saw her again.

One day (*don't recall when*) in 1958 they called for a photographer to report to the Western Air Defense Command Center War Room to record events as they unfolded. I was sent. I had a 35mm camera and was instructed to shoot the big board every 5 minutes unless things started getting hotter, then to record every minute. The big board is a gigantic two story plexiglass map of the entire Western United States. There were people behind it at various levels on scaffolding. These folks were all connected to head sets and would write things backwards on the big board with grease pencils on their side that appeared correct from the front side. The grease pencil writing glowed under black light. Today of course this is all a big computer board, but then it was all a man (or woman) operation. To the best of my memory it kept track of all military aircraft and military naval craft involved in the current operation over all the states west of the Continental Divide. ***{Note: It is no longer called ADC, it is now called the WADS (Western Air Defense Sector) and it encompass everything west of the Mississippi.}***

A Russian Sub was sitting at periscope depth just outside the Golden Gate Bridge and was blocking incoming and outgoing sea traffic. The US Navy Fleet was coming up from San Diego. The Coast Guard was circling the sub, ADC was scrambling every plane that could fly and SAC was on alert. There I was, stationed with my little 35mm camera shooting this activity from a position directly below the level where the Generals were talking about what they were going to do next. It was decided that the "Ruskeys" were there just to see what we would do. We apparently gave them one big show because he went "down scope" and scooted the hell out of there. The whole incident (*at least my involvement*) took a little less than four hours as I recall.

Pilots Lounge

Every time I had the day off *(well, maybe not every time, but many times!)* after pulling Alert Photographer I would hang around the Alert Pilots lounge and listen to their stories. In fact, on one occasion a pilot that had been flying chase down at Edwards AFB mentioned, "We must have some plane called Oh You Too, because I was in the "O Club" and a buddy said he was going to the big picnic and I casually remarked back "Oh, … You Too?" and all of a sudden two big guys grab me and I was interrogated a couple hours about what I know about an Oh You Too? (*It was very shortly after this that the whole world knew about U-2's and Frances Gary Powers*)

Hanging with the pilots was important to me. I had shot most of the pilots pictures with their aircraft and made a lot of good friends. I kept begging for a jet ride but I had to get ejection seat and altitude chamber cards before anyone would be allowed to take me up. It was a rule. My dream came true when a mission assignment required me to get the cards. I was to be the backup photographer for a photo mission in a F-104B *(a pilot trainer two seat version of the F-104 Star-fighter.)* Hamilton was to become the first operational base of the F-104. S/Sgt Ed Edwards was to be the primary and I was the secondary *(back-up)* photographer. We both had to go to Alameda Naval Air Station in San Francisco for the Altitude Chamber Training and Ejection Seat Training. It was great. The ejection seat was actually a near vertical ramp track on which your seat was propelled (*rapidly*) up the rails about 30 feet the instant you pulled the ejection sheet handle. When the cartage fires you are sent flying up at about 9 gazillion G's and it feels like your ass is left behind. The altitude chamber was made to take you to outer space and see if you could breathe there, which of course you can't, so you pass out! Critical training if you're ever in outer space and recognizing your passing out from being in a vacuum. But as a result of re-locating our kidneys and passing out in outer space we received our official US government certified USDA/BSA/CIA/LMNOP approved Altitude Cards and Ejection Seat cards. They were like gold to me and stayed with me all the time I was in the Air Force. It afforded me the opportunity to fly in the T-33(*there is a story coming up about that*!), several times in the F-100 Super Saber (*there is one story about that later!*), F-101 Voodoo, and TF-102A Delta Dart (*Here I sat beside the pilot not behind like in the other jets*) and a F-105 (*there is a story later about that too*!).

With my cards (*affectionately called tickets*) in hand I waved them in front of my two favorite pilots Capt. James "Jim" Smith and especially Capt. Walt Irwin who had just recently returned from Edwards flying chase on some (*classified*) research and test aircraft (*I'm guessing, but probably the Air Forces SR-71 Blackbird*). It was either he or Capt. Frank Belinne or possibly Capt. George Davis that told a story. Anyway, someone in the alert room told about shooting up to an altitude of 91,000 plus feet (*They were in a full contained pressurized suit and were breaking the existing altitude record*). If you are aware of the F-104 configuration, it is a long framed pointed aircraft with small stubby wings a high tail with the ailerons at the top of the tail. It was dubbed "the missile with a man in it." It was "all power" and the pilots said it had the glide ratio of a rock. One of them said "I started my climb with full MIL (*Military power*). At 75,000 the engine ran out of air and shut down but I have a lot of forward energy. As I approached the programed altitude to level off I pushed the stick forward. The aircraft does a slight nose over but is still going up. Then it is flat to the horizon and still going up, then tail up, but is still going **up**. I am in a totally uncontrolled non-flight condition. The ground is calling off altitude and telling me to level off, "*88.5 level off, 89 level off, 89, 500 level off, 90, 000 level off, 90,500 come on, … level off.*" She finally hangs there at 91,000 and a little bit for what seemed like a minute. I thought I was in orbit. I was in a slight nose down position when she decided to return to earth. I was (*obviously*) still in non flight, flat spin, but nose coming over more and more. No hydraulics, no engine start and I look out and see the edges of the wings starting to glow red and bits of metal melting and flying off. I don't know if it's me shaking violently or if it's the aircraft. Finally she comes alive again with an engine air start and I got back into controlled flight at around 20,000 feet."

Hamilton Tower 1-1-8

Hamilton AFB Flightline 1958

As I said, Capt. Irwin was my super favorite pilot and when I showed him my "tickets" he said, "Okay then, lets get you on a little familiarization flight." I think the other pilots knew what he meant, … I didn't. What he meant in coded talk was "I'll run him through the ringer."

The Captain checked out a T-bird (*T-33*) and I got a flight suit, g-suit and helmet with radio and oxygen mask. Jesus, … I was a real jet jockey. When I walked out to my "bird", helmet under my arm, in my gray AF flight suit and a g-suit over it I felt like I had to be the coolest guy on the planet. The Crew Chief got me all buckled in and carefully directed my attention to a tag attached to a pin down near my foot. "See this tag? As soon as you get out on the end of the runway you have <u>got to remember</u> to reach down and pull this pin. This pin is the safety for the arming of the ejection seat. If you don't pull the pin the seat won't fire, so it's <u>very import to do it</u>, understand? Do it just as soon as you are at the end of the runway and start the roll."

"Okay! Got it!" I said with a thumbs up and all the sincerity in the world, … but please, you have to forgive me. The best intentions got lost in the excitement of all that was going on. We taxied out, I am shooting pictures like mad, like I never saw a runway before. Well, I never did from a JET FIGHTER before (*albeit a trainer*). We started our roll, the afterburner kicks in and the acceleration is a kick in the ass! Zoom we're off and we climb out (as good as a T-33 could do) and it is just seconds we are at 10,000 feet. I know this because the Captain announces it on the radio to Hamilton tower "1 1 8 at 10 angels heading to Clear Lake to practice aerobatics." (*Note: in retrospect, some of today's commercial jet liner pilots take off at almost as steep an incline and nearly as fast a rate of climb as the T-33 did back then, but give me a break, it was this kids first jet ride!*)

I heard that! To practice aerobatics! ... Shit! I used to get sick on the marry-go-round and Ferris Wheel. But that was when I was a kid. My dad was a private pilot and he would take me flying in a Piper Cub and I would get deathly sick and throw up all over the interior of his airplane. But I was a kid then. It's different now, … right? Wrong!

It started when I was adjusting my camera (*looking at it*) and then I looked over the right side to shoot the ground. No ground, only blue sky. I quickly looked over to the left side, ... no ground, only blue sky. I slowly looked up through the canopy ... and there was the ground. We were flying upside down yet I had no sensation of it – well, … for those few seconds. Then the Capt started doing an eight point star snap roll and when we were in the up side down position again he does a snap nose over and we start a rapid, power, spinning on a center axis, dive – straight down. Then at the bottom there is a hard pull up that the g-suit begins inflating. (*Note: The purpose of the G-suit is to keep blood in your brain which helps prevent you from blacking out. It does this by inflating at your waist and lower abdomen forcing all your body parts up into your skull, the higher the G- force the more body parts. I think I feel my testicles pass by where my Adams apple used to be!*) After the pull up we are climbing straight vertical. He is giving the T-bird all the energy he can with the momentum and speed gained in the dive and full power on the climb with engine going full AB (*after burner*). Up - up we go, until the old bird just can't go no more and we came to a vertical stall. We fall back in a small upside down flat spin and he quickly regains a controlled flight condition once more. He said something to me but I don't answer. (*My mouth is filled with vomit!*) He is looking at me in the rear-view mirror and said "Is your radio out?" I shake my head no. "Your oxygen off?" I shake my head no again. "You're not sick are you?" I nod my head yes. "Oh God!" he said, "Don't throw up in your mask you'll drown in it! Is there a burp bag back there in the map rack on your left?" No burp bag. I shake my head no. "I don't have one up here either. Quick, open your mask, take off your shoe and spit it in there." He instructs.

The thought of that was disgusting so I just swallowed. "Never mind, Sir. I swallowed it!" I said.

There is a pause, "Oh shit, now THAT makes me sick!"

Apparently something we did in the last aerobatics must have knocked a radio wire lose somewhere in his radio that the radio between the Captain and the tower no longer worked. The intercom between us was fine and the radio between me and the tower was okay, so he would tell me what to say and I would click on the mike button and repeat what he said. (*sometimes almost close to verbatim!*) In one incidence he said to "Call Hamilton and say 1 1 8 at 24 angels above Clear lake heading back to base to shoot touch and go landings!"

"Roger" I said (*that is good military talk indicating the affirmative!*) and I clicked on the mike. Just then he does a hard bank right and a partial upside down back flip loop and heads towards Hamilton. The g-suit is inflating as I am trying to communicate. The grunting sound that came out of my mouth sounded something like, "Onnne...onnne....atttte.... dissss cizzz Ham...ill...ton.... at twenty … twenty four angels shooting..... shooting touch and go lan...dings above Clear, …. (*burp*) Lake!"

The Captain was laughing and after a moment of silence from Hamilton came, "What? This is Hamilton Tower, repeat 1 1 8?"

As we came back to base the Capt told me to call the tower and when he said "Now!" tell the tower "Hamilton, 1 1 8 on the break!" We came in over the Base directly above and in line with the runway and then when we were even with the tower on our left he said "Now!" and kicked it over hard bank left. A very hard left.

I made another one of those grunting calls to Hamilton "Ham ell ton ... onne, onne, eighate, onn the breakkk!) The g-suit was pushing my guts up in my throat and I know my testies are way up there. I ask to him as we leveled out "Whew.... how many G's was that?" He laughed and said "Oh - two or three." then he looks down at his g-meter and said "Five."

All good things must come to an end and so do terrifying ones. No seriously, this was really the most exciting day of my life to date. It had been a day I will always remember and cherish. As we were taxiing back to our parking area I saw the Crew Chief standing there with the ladder and suddenly remembered the pin used to arm the ejection seat that I had forgotten to pull. I reached down and pulled it just as the aircraft was coasting to a stop, the engine was whining down and the ladder was being attached. The Crew Chief popped his head in and looked down at my feet. He then patted me on the back as he slipped the pin back in saying, "Good Man! Most newbies forget to pull the pin on their first flight."

Other First

There were a lot of 'first' for me at Hamilton. One day, I was standing in the portrait studio looking out the window. From my position I can see the Air Police barracks across the street. It is a multistory concrete building and past that I can see down the street to the flight-line and distant hangers and buildings. All of a sudden I hear a very low rumble and way, way off, I see buildings sway and then ones closer bob up, then down. It is like a single wave but it is the ground that is moving, like a wave in the water. I blink and strain my eyes looking at this phenomenon. I have never seen anything like this. Suddenly the building across the street raises up and slams down and a split second later I am tossed up about a foot in the air as well as everything else in the room and we all come crashing down. The rumble ceases, the shake is over and we all were checking everyone. We are all okay. The totally amazing thing to me is, there was not a single crack to be found in the concrete or tile of the photo lab or was there any visible damage on base, yet I saw visible, physical, movement and bending of the unbend-able! I just experienced my first tiny earth tremor - a ground wave.

One of my other 'first' was to photograph an autopsy of a burned body. An interesting thing. I wasn't upset by the fact it was a person, that part amazingly didn't bother me, it just looked like meat even though I knew it was much more than that. What bothered me was the smell. When I worked for George Wisler he covered a really bad car/truck accident. The people had burned up in a fire. His equipment all came back with this odor that was very nauseating. This was that same stench and it permeated my equipment too. I could always tell you which camera I had used that day just by that smell.

One of my very good friends and photographers in the photo lab was A/3c (soon to become A/2c) John E. Brunner. Johnny, we called him, was single, but had a unique situation that permitted him to live off base. His father was the head electrician on the (then active) prison of Alcatraz and Johnny lived there with his dad. His parents were divorced. (*His mom lived in Southern California in San Diego I believe*) Every morning Johnny had to catch the first supply boat from the island to the mainland and drive thru part of San Francisco, cross the Golden Gate, up highway 101 to Hamilton. I'm guessing, but I would say it was a trip of 30 miles driving not counting the boat trip. If you know anything about famous highway 101 it probably has (*or at least had*) more accidents on it per mile than any highway in the USA. To capitalize on this, Johnny would stop and shoot pictures of the accidents going to and from work. He would leave a card and one or the other of the two (*or sometimes both*) of the owners insurance companies would buy prints and sometimes negatives from Johnny. He often made much more money a month doing that than he made in his AF pay. One morning he was way ahead of schedule, (*no accidents*) and he saw a CHP (*California Highway Patrol*) Officer on a motorcycle pull a guy over so Johnny decided to stop and watch what transpired. The Officer and the guy get in a tussle and the CHP Officer gets an arm lock, throws him over his cycle and calls for assistance. Johnny gets a shot of this and leaves. He takes the unprocessed film, (*he shot it on his personal Rollieflex*) to the top news paper in San Francisco, goes up to the photo editor and tells him what he has. He tells Johnny he is not interested. Dishearten, on his way to work he stops one last time at a small daily ***The News Call Bulletin*** and talks to the Editor, who gives him $10 for the unprocessed film. The Editor said he would process the film and if it was a slow day he might be able to run it. That night, Johnny was back on Alcatraz with his father and had totally forgotten about the picture. The phone rings and it's his mom calling from southern California. "Congratulations, I saw your picture in the paper today!" she said. Now if someone were to say they saw YOUR picture you think they are talking about a picture OF you. Johnny said, "You saw my picture in your paper? What for?" She said, "What? Oh, well maybe it is someone else with the same name." "Same name? What does it say?" Johnny asks. "It is a picture of a police officer with a guy across his motorcycle calling for help and it said at the bottom AP Wire Photo by John E. Brunner." Johnny received a $50 check from AP for their use of his photo and $25 from Life Magazine for future use rights and in 1958 that was a lot of bucks. But wait, … the story isn't over.

Sometime during the next month Johnny received a check in the mail for $350 and a letter announcing his photo won "Best AP and UPI Photo of the Month of November." Now in 1958 you could buy a fairly decent used car for all the money he's raked in from this one picture! The Base Public relations department even did an article on Johnny about the picture and there was a story in the base paper with a picture of Johnny holding a 16x20 of his now 'famous' photograph. Good old Capt King was quoted as saying "It's ironical that the most successful shot he ever made was on his off duty time."

Major Wire Services Term Base Fotog's Shot Best For November

A/2C John E. Brunner turned out to be "Johnnie on the Spot" last week when his timely picture of a San Francisco motorcycle patrolman's tussle with a reckless driver won him national recognition from two major news associations and LIFE magazine.

Brunner, a photographer assigned to the Base Photo Lab, was driving south on US 101 on the evening of Nov. 30, when he saw Officer David Ansuriza pin a speeding driver, Edgar A. Whitehead of South San Francisco across his motorcycle.

TOP PICTURE OF NOV.

Johnnie shot his classic picture with the Rolleiflex he keeps handy in his car, and headed back to San Francisco. Although one city newspaper didn't want the film, he found a ready buyer in the NEWS CALL-BULLETIN who sold the picture to both the Associated Press and the United Press-International. Both wire services agreed it was the outstanding news picture of November for both of them as the shot made front page headlines throughout the United States.

In addition to the original $10 he received from the NEWS CALL-BULLETIN, Brunner was paid $50 from the AP and UPI for using the picture, $25 from LIFE Magazine for future use of the negative, and finally 350 more from AP and UPI for being judged the best news photo of November—he squeezed it in 30 minutes before Dec. 1.

Brunner, who was on leave at the time, knew he had hit pay dirt when he spotted his picture Dec. 1 as a front pager in the San Diego TRIBUNE.

Five years ago, Johnnie nearly scooped all the papers with his shot of a girl swimming around Alcatraz. This picture sold to local papers, but did not stir up the interest the motorcyclist vs. driver did.

RECEIVES PROMOTION

Only 19 years old, Johnnie returned from his leave to find himself promoted to Airman Second Class, and the pride of the Photo Lab. His boss, Capt. Robert King, remarked 'It's ironical that the most successful shot he ever made, was on his off duty time."

Future plans for Brunner, who lives on Alcatraz Island with his father, is to get into criminal investigation work. With his knack for getting there "firstest with the mostest", we say he'll succeed!

His historic picture appeared in national papers which included: the New York TELEGRAM SUN: New York DAILY NEWS: New York DAILY MIRROR; New York HERALD TRIBUNE:

ALL THIS AND A Promotion Too beams A/2C John E. Brunner of the Base Photo Lab after his epic picture won him top awards from two national news wire services. Here he holds part of the $1' he earned with his timely photo. The stripes he's wearing are s of an extra bonus as a result of his promotion Dec. 1.

(While it sounds like a prickish thing to say, the truth is he is really covering the fact that Johnny was actually on a duty day. If it were discovered he was "Officially on duty" the picture could in fact be property of the Air Force. So he wasn't really being nasty!) (*See clipping from base paper – Note, while it said he was on leave – he was actually coming to work, but it was his "off duty time" – before he was due for work that this all occurred.*) Wait - wait, … the story doesn't end there!

Months pass, Johnny gets a letter. "Dear Mr. Brunner," It begins, "We regret to inform you your photograph titled "Call for backup" came in second place for the Pulitzer Prize in Photography for 1958. The prize this year went to William C. Beall of the Washington Daily News for his photograph "Faith and Confidence" showing a policeman patiently reasoning with a two-year-old boy trying to cross a street during a parade. Johnny has the letter framed in his office even today. How's that for a pretty close call to a touch with fame.

Tyndall AFB

July 1958 I was sent on a 90 day TDY (*Temporary Duty Assignment*) to Tyndall AFB, Panama City Florida, to support "Operation William Tell." It was an ADC (Air Defense Command) shooting contest where all the ADC wings in the AF come and shoot at targets from their aircraft. I think we (*Hamilton AFB*) flew F-86 Sabers at that time. (*Soon to become the first operational base for the F-104 Star-fighter*) Because I got this plum assignment TDY I was unable to go before the Promotion board that convened while I was away. T/Sgt Merrill Myers stood in for me before the board and she told me later I had all sorts of support from the Lab Chief as well. I had already taken and passed the 5.0 Level test for photographer so I was up on everything I needed to get promoted. Needless to say I got a call from Sgt Merrill Myers informing me I was promoted to A/2c. I got to put my new stripes on at Tyndall.

I was assigned to work in the color transparency processing lab. Another fellow assigned there was A/1c Earl Dunnick. We hit it off like

long lost brothers and palled around after duty hours. The work schedule was 12 hours on and 12 off so there wasn't a lot of off duty fun time but we managed. One event at the Airman's Club had strippers performing that went all the way. Earl and I were down front getting pictures of all this of course. The next day we processed the film along with the official AF stuff and was secretly showing it around to the guys in the Photo Lab. That same day the Base Commander talked to the Airman Wives Club and according to the article in the base paper said, "I know you have heard rumors that there will be wild parties with strippers. Nothing could be further from the truth. I guarantee that no such parties will happen on my base." He said this while speaking from the very stage that naked women were dancing on the night before. Earl and I quickly destroyed our evidence to the contrary. (*There were some really good closeups too!*)

Shortly after that I was assigned to work at the Press Camp. Which meant I shot pictures not printing them. I also was on an eight hour work schedule, albeit seven days a week (*Rather the twelve hour the guys in the Lab were on.*) There I had the real adventures of Tyndall AFB. I am not exactly sure of the sequence of the following events, which happen first, second, etc., but essentially it went like this.

The Base Information Officer (*IO*) wanted a picture of the Tyndall AFB tower with a F-106 flyby at a height lower than the top of the tower. They had drawings of what they wanted and it was to be the cover of the Base Phone Book. The F-106 was scheduled to be deployed at Tyndall shortly (*After Operation William Tell*). The Air Force didn't "own" F-106's yet, they were still in the Aircraft manufacturers inventory and not officially signed over to the Air Force. The manufacturer sent a F-106 to Tyndall (*out from nearby Eglin AFB that was there for testing*), just for the photo mission and it was only to be a one time, one pass, fly-by! The IO had a platform that was approximately 30 feet high assembled and placed on a flat bed truck. The truck was stationed out in the grass about 30 yards off the edge of the runway in front of the tower. Attached at the top of the platform were two sheets of 3/4" plywood. There was no railing, because we needed to have an unobstructed view. At the appointed time the IO and I climbed to the top. Even going up it wobbled – a lot! I am not afraid of heights, but I must admit that being on the top of the platform was severely frightening. I could tell the Lt was equally concerned and neither of us stood up. We were as low to the plywood as we could get. The Lt had a walkie-talkie radio between him and the tower and he told them we were set. I had pre-focused, exposure adjusted with the shutter set on 1/1000th of a second. Film holder inserted and dark slide pulled, I was ready. We waited for about five minutes and then the tower called and said the F-106 was starting his run. The IO looking around, looked off in the direction of Panama City and said (*I quote*) "Oh shit! He lit up afterburners." Off in the far distance I could make out a tiny puff of smoke and a dot approaching us at what we can call a high rate of speed. I was trying to follow him in my sports finder panning with him. Allowing for reaction time I fired my shutter just as he reached the area of the tower and I followed through with my panning as he zoomed by.

"Hold on!" screamed the Lt! Just then we were struck with a sonic boom. The platform tower we were on, was knocked backwards. The platform seemed to hang for the longest time in a position that I'm sure if it went back another foot it would have been past the balance point and would have gone on over. Then it bounced forward to nearly the same critical balance point. After hanging there a moment it proceeded to go back and then forth in shorter and shorter osculations finally settling down. I am convinced that if the platform had not been firmly attached to the flatbed of the truck it would have gone over. (*Had we been standing we would have been goners.*) All the time this is going on the Lt is shouting obscenities and we are holding on for dear life. (*That is not to say I wasn't saying anything – quite frankly I am sure if I did, I was screaming like a little baby!*) The postmortem to this is the picture was framed perfect, but the F-106 was a long blur and even at 1/1000th of a second my fast pan to catch the aircraft blurred as also was the tower. It was useless. As an aftermath of this the tower lost one window and several windows all along the flight line were shattered.

The runway at Tyndall lines up with the main street of Panama City and the 106's run caused sever damage in downtown. Several plate glass windows were broken or cracked along the street and the Air Force had to pay hundreds of thousands of dollars in damages. Our base photographers had to go shoot pictures of all claims against the Air Force. There were a lot of broken window or missing window pictures taken. It was pure luck that no one was severely hurt in the city or base. I don't know what happened to the "civilian" that was piloting the F-106. I would assume he was fired.

A Job gone silly

The following story is absolutely true. I couldn't make up such a story. Being at the press camp I was often sent out to shoot a couple shots of some activity happening on the flight line. We had been issued brand new Linhof 4x5 press camera and three lenses, A wide angle, normal and telephoto. If my mission only called for me to shoot a couple wide angle shots that is all I took. Here is where the fun starts. I'm walking down the flight line and my Base Commander, Col Celears is standing next to his aircraft, see's me and calls out, "Airman Voris, come over here please." Of course I do and he explains he needs a picture of himself standing next to his plane. He explains how he wants it framed on him, indicating with his hands slightly above his head and down to his mid chest, "and get some of the aircraft in the picture." he said. I recognize exactly what he want and because I had the wide angle lens on (*and that was the only lens I had with me*) I started walking up real close. "No, no!" he said and reexplains what he wants.

I respond with "Yes Sir, I understand, it's just...."

I am interrupted before I can explain about the lens. "Back up, back up!" he said.

"Yes Sir. Where would you like me to stand, Sir." He direct me to a place that would probably be a good location if I had a normal lens on the camera. Once he was satisfied with my position I shot the picture, labeled the holder and would later have it sent to the Photo Lab who would see that the prints got to my Base Commander. I proceeded on to my assigned mission. Well, of course the lab doesn't crop the picture, they send a full frame shot and it shows Col Celears full figure, his entire aircraft and half the flight line.

Wait – the story is not over!

A couple days later, same flight line, same scenario. The Col calls me over to his aircraft and said he got the picture but it wasn't what he wanted and carefully re-explained the framing with one hand above his head and the other at his waist. Unfortunately, I only had the telephoto on the camera and no other lens with me. (*Honest!*) I said I understood what he wanted and started to back up when he said, "No, no, come forward, come closer and proceeds to re-explained the framing he wanted.

"Sir, I understand but, ..."

I'm interrupted again with "Come closer!"

I did as I was told, asking, "Where would you like me to stand, Sir!" He positions me way to close, but being the obedient solder I shot the picture from where he said. It was an excellent closeup of his chubby face.

(*You might have been able to make out that there was a fussy part of an airplane behind his ear.*)

Wait, wait... it's not over! (*I promise this is all absolutely true!*)

The very next afternoon I am going down the flight line and there, low and behold, is my Base Commander Col Celears out by his aircraft. He spots me, calls me over and tells me about the picture he just received and that it wasn't what he wanted. He ask me (*amazingly calm I will add*) if I could shoot a picture of him cropped like, indicating with his hands slightly above his head and down to his mid chest, "and get some of the front of aircraft in the picture? Ohh and you can stand anywhere you want, just can you get me the damn picture!"

I told him of course, and it so happened I had a normal lens on the camera that day. I stood at the approximate distance he originally had directed me to stand when I had the wide angle lens on the camera. I know he figured I was messing with him, but he got the picture he wanted and commented on it to me occasionally when I shot pictures in his office back at Hamilton. He would say to whom ever we were shooting pictures with him, "Don't try to tell this young Airman where to stand." (*It was a private joke.*)

One morning I decided to go swimming before work at the base beach. It was just daybreak and the gulf water was calm as glass. I had purchased fins, snorkel and mask, but never had used them. In fact, even the swimsuit was new. I was alone and there was not another sole on the beach. I entered the water and it was delightful. It was very shallow and it was almost a hundred yards from shore before it started to drop off much.

As the bottom began to drop off I thought I could make out a couple logs on the bottom in about 10 feet of water. I figured I'd try and dive down and investigate. As I got close I could make out that the logs were not logs, they were in reality, ... SHARKS! Each about 6 foot long. Do you have any idea how difficult it is to swim backwards with swim-fins and keeping your eye on two dark objects in the water for a hundred yards. I think I was still going backwards when I was up on the beach. I never went in the water the rest of the time I was in Florida!

Speaking of mornings at Tyndall AFB, I'd start off walking to the chow hall for breakfast and if the wind was coming from the north the whole base was saturated with the awful odor of the paper mill. That would turn the strongest of stomach's. I don't think I ate ten percent of my breakfast's there.

Marriage Preparation & back at the Press Camp

I was getting married to Melanie at the end of my 90 day TDY at Tyndall. She was a Catholic and I was a Baptist. Because we were getting married in her Catholic Church I needed to take Catholic Instruction. The Air Force Base Catholic Chaplin provided this service, in fact I was given an hour off every few days to go see the Chaplin. It was an excellent one on one time and I always looked forward to it. We talked about theology of course but also about sex! You can imagine my surprise when a Catholic Chaplin Priest told me "It okay for your wife to place your penis in her mouth to make it hard!" Now that was a cool guy!

In addition to the Catholic instruction I also needed a blood test to get married. I was never one to wait until the last minute so I had my blood test early. Too early as I come to discover. I went to the Base Hospital to request the blood test which they of course provided. I never had easy veins to hit and I was given a corpsman that I might have been his second blood draw. After stabbing me a couple dozen times on one arm he proceeded to try the other arm. Finally he hit pay dirt. When I got up to leave I suddenly felt lightheaded and grabbed a wall stud. (*Note: The Hospital was exposed open interior stud walled with exterior wood siding.*) I closed my eyes and it felt like someone whopped me on the back of the head. I also thought I was still holding on to the wall stud. I wasn't. I was flat on my back and when I became aware of my surroundings a couple corpsman were standing over me asking me if I was alright. They were laughing over the fact I passed out having my blood taken for getting married. As I mentioned earlier, I goofed. I did it too soon. It has to be within 30 days of marriage. I ended up having to go back and repeat the process. I went back the second time assuming it would be a repeat of my previous visit but this time I got the slickest blood drawer in the hospital. She, a WAF this time, was in and out before I was even aware she drew blood.

Back on the flight line, an F-102 came back from a firing mission with one missile stuck half out of his missile bay. (*I should explain that the F-102 had internal weapon bays to carry both guided missiles and rockets. The doors of the two forward bays each had tubes for 12 FFAR (a total of 24) 2.75 in (70 mm) rockets. The whole rack or bay carrying the air-to-air missiles drops down below the aircraft and after the rockets are fired the bay is retracted back into the aircraft's belly. That is the normal – optimal - function.*) As I said, here was this "Deuce" (*The name the F-102 was often given.*) with a missile half out of the rack, the rack was retracted so the rocket was crunched and bent down and the bay doors are partially closed. It looks like a tiny "penis" on this big bird. A deadly one at that. The tip of the rocket was mere inches off the runway. As the F-102 was taxiing back to it's parking place a crew chief saw what had happen and flagged the pilot to stop. He grabbed a ladder and told the pilot to shut down and get out immediately, which he did. The immediate area was evacuated and then the following scenario takes place. This is where I enter the picture.

Being assigned on the flight line was "like" being the alert photographer so I hopped in a jeep and went with the FSO (*Flying Safety Officer*) out to where the "Deuce" was sitting. A crew chief had subsequently wired up a long cable line to the cockpit to be able to remotely open the bay doors and drop the rack down. (*Which would bring the tip of the rocket in contact with the concrete runway.*) Everyone is back about a hundred feet and the FSO said to me, "Can you get a straight on shot of that as it comes down?"

I look at the FSO with a totally blank stare for a couple seconds and then without changing expression offer him the camera. He nods and said, "Yeah, … that's a pretty dumb idea!" Well, the rack came down, no explosion, the rocket didn't ignite, nor was there any major damage to the aircraft. I shot pictures of Ordnance Disposal removing the rocket, with the telephoto I might add. Then the closeup aircraft damage after it was towed back to it's hanger, and later the rocket (*after it was made inert and safe.*) See, I was beginning to be a little more cautious and think about safety.

Damn #22 Flash Bulbs

The grand finality of Operation William Tell is of course the announcement of the top guns and the awarding of the trophies. The winners of the 1958 Operation William Tell would receive their awards from the Chief of Staff of the US Air Force, (*Four Star*) General Thomas Dresser White, who was only the fourth Air Force Chief of Staff to date. Tyndall's Base Commander Col Richard T. Kight was a famous man in his own right. He had been the personal pilot to the Vice President of the United States Henry Wallace, President Roosevelt and for many other dignitaries. I was assigned to cover the arrival of General White. I was told that if I didn't get any other picture I must be sure to get a shot of the General stepping out of the door of his aircraft waving and one at the bottom of the steps as he shakes hands with the Base Commander, Col Kight. Well, the plane arrived at dusk. Of course there is a lot of fanfare, including a band, lines of troupes to review. The Base Commander and his staff were standing at the base of the steps. The door opened and the General stepped out and gave a wave. I clicked the shutter, but the %^$# flash bulb didn't fire and it's too dark to get an existing light exposure. By then he started to descend the steps and I gave an audible groan. The General stopped and asked, "Did you need that picture son?"

"Yes Sir!" I responded.

He said "Okay!" and stopped, turned around and went back up steps to go inside the aircraft's door. Now get the picture of what is going on here. There are all these people watching this transpire, the band started playing the moment he first appeared at the aircraft door, but now that he has gone back inside the aircraft they don't know what to do. Some continue playing, some stop, it becomes total confusion and disarray. The band suddenly sounded like a Junior High marching band all playing on a different page of sheet music.

The General announces "Ready?"

"Yes Sir!" I respond. I had taken the bulb out and licked the tip. (*This helps improve the conductivity*) He stepped out and waved, the band started up again, I click the shutter and NOTHING – no flash again!

"We'll give it one more try son." and returns to be inside his aircraft. The band now sounds like a grade school orchestra tuning up.

By now I'm shaking. I remove the bulb, put in a new one and pray it isn't the batteries. I was sure it wasn't batteries because I had installed all new one's in the flash gun. I announced, "Okay Sir!" and out he came, waving, smiling like MacArthur arriving at the Philippines. The band begins again, for the third time, the shutter CLICKS and the FLASH **FIRES!** Thank God! I had a new film holder in dark slide pulled and a fresh bulb in by the time he reached the bottom of the steps and grasped the hand of the Base Commander. I would love a copy of that picture to show you. It was a great shot of General White but Col Kight looked like he was in shell shock. (*You know Col Kight wanted to kill me. My only explanation is that General White must have had indicated to someone down the chain of command that he wanted a picture of himself waving as he was exiting his Aircraft.*) The rest of the coverage of General White's stay went as smooth as clockwork. And was told later that I got some great shots. No other bulb failed to fire. It just had to be that first bulb! (*Another good example why we needed electronic flash units*!)

Wedding

Note this poor quality picture is the only picture we have of our wedding party as George Wisler had a "paying" job the day of our wedding.

On November 2nd I was able to get a military "hop" on a transport out of Tyndall to Wright Patterson AFB. I had a two week leave to get married. It was set for November 8th, 1958 in St Josephs Catholic Church and the reception at the Kerr Dean Inn, about the fanciest place in Springfield Ohio at the time. Melanie had just turned 17 on October 30th and I was 19 going on 20 in four months (*March 4th*) We honeymooned at the Lincoln Lodge in Columbus Ohio *(Oh - by the way my dear wife in "proof reading" this, reminded me that she paid for the honeymoon – which I don't recall at all. But I am sure that is absolutely true since that would be something a woman would never forget! (or forgive?))* We had to sneak a 6 pack of Miller Beer into our room to celebrate. Remember Melanie was only 17 and I was 19. (*We carried around one of those unopened bottles for years until it got so grungy and disgusting looking inside we finally tossed it.*)

At the end of our "honeymoon" I got a another "hop" to California via Wright-Patterson AFB to Huston Texas, then on to Edwards AFB and finally to Hamilton AFB (*2 day trip*) in prop transports bucket-seats. Melanie had to stay in Ohio to finish her High School Senior Year. In truth she had been thrown out of school because she "got married." Which in those days meant that everyone knew she had "officially done it!" (*Which nearly everyone in high school had already "done it" - just not officially!*) Well, Melanie's mother was, at the time, somewhat of a socialite in the community. Melanie's mom would not hear of them removing her daughter from school just for getting married. She went to the school board and let them have it. They decided to let Melanie back in school quick-time. Interestingly though, it was "discovered" that by the end of the winter semester, Melanie had sufficient credits to graduate and her High School Diploma would be mailed to her. (*In-other-words- don't come back Spring Quarter!)* Well, Melanie wasn't the least upset by this turn of events and was certainly ready to get on with being the little loving housewife.

Meantime, I was back at Hamilton and bought a 1947 Dodge sedan. (*We called her the Blue Bolt.*) I was being sent TDY to Lowry AFB, Denver Colorado to the Air Force Color Photography Processing School. I was permitted to take a weeks advance leave to get Melanie in Ohio and come back to Denver to begin my advanced training. It was an 8 week school.

In Ohio, we gathered up our wedding presents, packed the "Blue Bolt" and said our goodbys to family and friends. We quickly headed off to Denver and the Air Force to begin our life's adventure.

First off, be aware that my sweet young, inexperienced Melanie had never been out of the State of Ohio, and not much farther than her own Clark County. As we crossed the Ohio/Indiana State line I proudly announced, "Well kitten, we're in Indiana now!"

She is looking about with a very doubtful expression on her face and said ,"Untt Aaa! No we're not!" I wondered what brought that on and asked her why she thought we weren't in Indiana? She proudly announced, "Because Ohio is green on the map and Indiana is Yellow!"

I didn't know how I was going to explain Illinois not being purple!

In Denver, Melanie and I found a little one and a half room apartment that was across the street from Mamie Eisenhower's Mothers house on Oak Street. (*Melanie is the one that said she is sure of this – I don't recall the street name. I think she's wrong, and that Mamie's mom lived a few blocks down the street from our apartment.*) It was winter and I remember it got cold enough to be among the few times I ever wore my AF horse blanket full-length coat.

We were so poor on my Military pay. Melanie worked at a Denver hospital as a nurses aide to help out financially, but we also had fun. In February 1959 I went to the Lowry Personal Services and checked out a toboggan, ski's, boots, polls, tent, cook stove, two sleeping bags, gas lantern

– we are ready for the wilds of Colorado and head off into the mountains for a weekend.

Ever heard of Frazier, Colorado? We inexperienced youngsters, never watched the weather reports (*no TV – couldn't afford one*) to notice that Frazier, Colorado is ofter the coldest spot in the nation and almost always the coldest in Colorado. It was February! I wondered why no one else had checked-out any of the camping gear from Personal Services. I thought that maybe I might be early and the first one to do so. (*I was, … about 4 months early!*) Anyway, Melanie and I find this neat logging road going up along the side a mountain outside the little town of Frazier and we take it. It is a dangerious drive and often the road is not much wider than the car with drop-offs of hundreds of feet. We reached a small flat area, the first we came to and decided this is where we would camp. It is wide enough to pull the car off the road and pitch the tent. There are even a few scrub pine trees around. It is actually a beautiful day with the sun shining. In the high 40's or low 50's and to young folks dressed warmly, that is fine weather. The tent was pitched we have explored and horsed around like lovers do. We try to get the cook stove going but realize we don't have white gas. There was a little in the lantern , but when we try to light the mantels the match touched the ash and they crumble and we are unable to get them to work. (*Neither of us have EVER use any of this stuff before.*) Melanie had some birthday candles in her purse and as it got dark that was our only source of light. As the sun dropped so did the temperature. In fact it was a race to see which would be the winner. The sun to total darkness or the temperature to a gazillion degrees below zero. It was a dead heat, but heat was NOT the operative word.

We ran out of candles and after putting one sleeping bag inside another hoping that two together would be warm enough, coupled with our body heat to get us through the night. It was just barely after dark, we hadn't eaten, we are cold, dirty, tired and did I mention freezing! But as tight as it was in the sleeping bag our feet was still ice cold and we were miserable. About 9:00 I heard a rustling outside the tent and sat up. I peered out the tent flap and there, in the dim starlight, were five Coyotes lined up outside the tent - like they were waiting in line for a meal, … us! I gave a loud cough and they took off running, but I had no idea how far. That was it, we were going to get out of here. We could leave the stuff and come back tomorrow and get it. We would drive back down the mountain get a nice warm motel for the night.

Hah!

I woke up Melanie and (*not telling her about the Coyotes – I didn't want her to freak out*) I said, "Come on honey, lets go down to a motel, it is to damn cold, we will freeze to death here." Shivering she agreed and we headed for the car. I had a hunting knife following up the rear and as Melanie got in the car she asked what that was for. That was when I told her about the Coyotes. We were glad we were in the safety of the car and now ready to start the car and drive down to a motel.

"Click gurnnnn, … Click" - That was the total sound the car gave in response to turning the key. Everything was frozen. We looked at each other in total panic. We were stuck on this frigging mountain top, in the car surrounded by Coyotes. (*Well, … to us we were!*) We failed to take the sleeping bags with us and rather than "risk the attack of the pack of coyotes" decided not to go back and get them. (*Okay - I know now they are more afraid of you than you are of them.*) But rather than risk it, we ripped the seat covers off and wrapped ourselves up together and – somehow – survived the night.

The next morning was followed with even dumber acts of stupidity on my part. (*Give me a break. I was 19 years old!*) I saw or read somewhere that in Alaska they heated under the car motor to get the engine oil to flow. I reasoned if it worked there it should work for us. Why I thought I should build a bonfire I have no idea. Why I should build it out of pine boughs (*because they cut off easy from surrounding scrub pine?*) I haven't a clue. Worse, why I should use an accelerate (*with the little remaining white gas in the lantern*) to facilitate its burning might be another poignant question. Regardless, that is what I did, … with the able assistance of my dear wife I might add. With my pine forest all wet down with white gas, neatly set up under the engine block/transmission area, I ignited my warmer.

Holy Shit! Flames were leaping higher than the top of the car. I had the hood up and the engine was completely enveloped in flames. I had to do something in a hurry. Melanie took off the break and guided the car as I pushed it off the fire. This meant of course that I had to walk through the fire I built. (*Note- here several points to consider: #1: The car for some reason did not catch on fire and explode as it probably should have or would have if it were a modern car model and #2: I want to give a reminder about the place we were camped and emphasize that car was precariously close to a straight drop-off. In fact when Melanie stopped the car she was unable to get out of the passenger side door because there was no room to stand before the cliff's shear 100 foot straight down drop. And finally #3: By some miracle I had the strength to push the car and did in fact manage to walk across (or through or over ?) the fire I built - that surely must have died down considerably. Okay you can call me Fire-walker from here on!*) After realizing how really stupid that was we came to recognize that our only option was to pack the car with the gear and walk back down the mountain. Fortunately, after about five miles we came upon a house that, based on the existence of telephone poles and lines, had electricity and telephone.

Now get this picture. Two waifs, filthy dirty from their ordeal, Melanie's hair looks like Medusa only worse and with more snakes show up on your door step on a Sunday morning. They appear from the middle of nowhere, no car, no back-pack, no bike, and they start babbling on about being stranded, car dead on the mountain, fire under it, blab, blab, blab. Do you shoot them, (*Colorado has very liberal gun laws*) or do you let them in?

Fortunately they did, the latter one, … and even called a tow truck for us. Melanie ask to use the bathroom and while she was there saw a brush and decided to borrow it to brush her hair. She was shocked to see how filthy the peoples brush was – then realized she was the cause of it being so dirty. We were given coffee as I recall maybe even breakfast. Finally the tow truck arrived and I went with the driver up the mountain. Several times his dual wheels had one set hanging partly over the edge of the drop off as the other side was scraping the edge of the cliff vertical walls. He said a few cuss words on the way up. When we got to my car we had to have him push me backwards to a spot where it was wide enough for him to pass by. Then he went on up the logging road (*I don't know how far but he was gone about 15 minutes*) so he could find a spot to turn around. When he came back he hooked on to me and pulled me not more than 20 feet and the ol' Blue Bolt fired up. We stopped back at the cabin to settle up. He was aware I was in the Air Force and a low ranking poor Airman.

"You are aware this is Sunday, right – week-end rates?" He said.

"Yes Sir." I saw the dollars flying.

"And the fact I had to come all the way around the mountain from Fraser to get here?"

"Yes Sir." More dollars piling on.

"Not to mention how dangerous it was for me to take my truck up that road. Why, my wheels were off the edge sometimes!" He pointed out.

"Yes Sir." I was starting to think I may have to give him Melanie.

"Hows $10.00" and winks at the folks that had been our hosts.

"Oh my God, thank you Sir, thank you." With the conclusion of this adventure I discovered that God most assuredly looks after fools and children. We were fully qualified on both accounts and God must surely have a sence of humor.

As if that wasn't enough!

Remember we still had all that ski equipment and had to go back over Berthoud Pass to get back to Denver. That was the big ski lift resort then and back then a G.I. and his dependent could ride the lift for a dollar each. (*Did I mention that Melanie and I had never skied before? We had never even had skis on our feet before and had to be shown how to attach them by some helpful folks.*) Should we go to the bunny hill and try them out? Ohh hell no! Get on the lift. After all it's just down hill, and I have been on a sled, how much different could it be? And we didn't have that much time left in the day so we have to get going.

I won't go into the total fiasco of us getting into the chair, I am sure your imagination can take care of that. Suffice it to say it did not match the graceful gliding up to the spot on your skis and gently setting back into the chair as it swung around to meet you. It looked so easy the way those other couples were doing it. Melanie and I were sure we had it all timed out. **Not!** I'm not sure but I think it was the third chair we managed to hang on to. The ride up to the top of the mountain was beautiful. That alone was well worth the dollar and the bruises. (*Including those sustained in the process of getting out of the chair lift.*) Are you aware that those things do not stop to let you off - you have to jump. Actually if you are practiced in the process you can just ski off gracefully, but if you stay on too long – especially after it makes the turn to go back down - the drop starts getting further and further!

We leaped off before it made the full turn but it wasn't a good landing as I recall. After collecting ourselves together and checking our gear, poles etc, we scooted over where people were zooming past us and shooting down the mountain. From this position we could barely make out the club house and where the ski lift started. It looked almost straight down – very similar to the mountain we almost pushed the car off of. I looked at Melanie, Melanie looked at me. For once the little voice in our heads got through to us and was screaming, "***ARE YOU OUT OF YOUR FREAKING MIND – YOU DON'T KNOW HOW TO SKI!***" I scooted backward a bit – so did she. I went farther, so did she. I bent down and unbuckled my bindings, she was doing the same. Do you know it's a lot easier to get on those chair lifts carrying your skis than it is if you're wearing them? The ride down was even more spectacular than the ride up. To this day I have never set foot in another pair of skis.

It should be the end of a hell of a weekend but my hell hadn't begun yet. We got back to Denver and I checked all the stuff back in on Base at Personal Services and we were home by six. As memory serves, I started having symptoms by eight and we went to the Base Hospital at about ten. I was admitted and spent the next five days in quarantine with an highly infectious pneumonia. Melanie didn't have a drivers license. The "Blue Bolt" had somehow lost its ability to go in reverse. There she was, a 17 year old kid, in a strange town, that had only been to the Base a couple times and has always been "directionally challenged" (*I swear that sometimes she gets confused on which way is "up"!*) She has to get home so through my fog of raging fever (*I get delirious when I have a fever over 100*) I explain how to get home and that she has to find a place to park that she doesn't have to back up. (*It would help if you would stop laughing at this point*) She left (*crying*) and luckily finds our street and our house but there is no place to park closer than several blocks from the house. But that will do for her. That is where the car goes. It is left there all the time I am in the hospital. Melanie rides the bus to work and she calls the base each day to find out when I can be seen. (*I am kept in total isolation – it must have been the bug from outer space!*) Finally, after 5 days I got to see Melanie, who would come out to base on the bus, and two days later I was released back to duty. I had been out 7 days so I was washed back in my training a week but it didn't count against me as a negative sence it was medically related. Just another little side trip in our little saga.

The mountains were a magnet to us. Every weekend we would head up to the foothills to enjoy that magnificent vista. But keep in mind it was still the winter. One such Sunday we decided to go to see "St Mary's Glacier"

We start up this plowed road and get to a plowed parking lot at a place that indicates it is a Dam that provides water for Denver. It is a beautiful sunny day, no body else around, the lake behind the dam is frozen. Right up against the dam you could see that water had melted and refroze. It was all like glass and very – very thick. You could see it was probably 3 or 4 foot thick. Even at that, we are gingerly testing and testing as we venture farther and farther out up next to the dam. Like I said, glass, super slick! - not another soul. We have thick wool socks on so we take our shoes off and find that if you slowly start running and build up speed you can slide, and slide and slide, like you have never slid in your life. We were having a ball. The laughter and screams echoed off the dams steep concrete wall. After an half an hour of this fun, (*We are up near the concrete and out in the center of the dam at this time.*) all of sudden there is an earsplitting roar and "crack" sound (*amplified by being next to the dam wall*) interrupts our play. From the center of the lake a huge crack was developing and heading our way along with a geyser of water shooting 10 feet into the air. Melanie took off in a dead run for the bank like she had steel cleats on her feet and on the way scooped up her shoes. She was safely on the bank before my little chubby feet could find any traction at all. All I was doing was running in place. (*very fast I might add!*) I learned that day that Melanie looks after Melanie. Ohh, as to what happened to me? My feet got wet, I slipped on the water/ice mixture and fell down, getting my pants wet. I drove back to town in my underwear. (*Blue Bolt had a GOOD heater thank heavens.*) On the way down the mountain, heading back to Denver, a Highway Patrol officer pulled us over because my California plates had expired. (*I had a tag in my window that said the plates had been renewed but the State of California was delayed in issuing new plates. It said exactly where to display the tag in the window – which I did.*) The officer read the tag but also noticed I was in my underwear and barefoot. I was of course excused for the license plate but told in no uncertain terms "to get my clothes and shoes on" in order to drive a car. "Yes Sir!" I was quick to comply. No ticket was issued but I am sure he had totally the wrong idea.

There was another incident about the expired license plate worthy of tale. I had been left a "warning" on the windshield that my out of state license plates had expired and I had 24 hours to get Colorado plates or my car would be towed to the impound lot. I ignored it of course, because I was following the California law and had placed the tag in the prescribed position. Melanie and I were sitting in our half kitchen at our half table playing cards when she noticed out the window there is a cop directing a tow truck to hook up our car. I am in my skivvies, but there isn't a moment to lose, I garbed a towel and wrapped it around me and rush out just before the tow truck drove off. I shout, "What do you think you're doing officer?"

"I left a warning ticket on this car yesterday that you had expired plates and if you didn't get Colorado plates it would be towed. Time's up!" he said with an arrogant tone.

"It is not expired!" I said and tapped the tag on the windshield."

He cautiously looked at the tag (*obviously noticed for the first time*) and carefully read it. Then said with a snide response, "Doesn't matter, this car has been here over 30 days and you have to get Colorado plates."

"Not if you are in the military! Notice the base stickers on the bumper, one is Hamilton AFB - California, my home base and one is Lowry AFB – which is here in Denver. I am in school here. Put - the – car - back!" I said and turned around and went back in the house. (*Actually I was freezing!*) I ran up stairs and Melanie was at the window. I told her the exchange of words and watched the Officer direct the tow truck operator carefully place the ol' Blue Bolt back in her parking place. A few minutes later there is a knock at the door and the Officer (*humble now*) asks if I will sign off on the ticket that he has had to 'rescind' and he needed my acknowledgment. Ahhh sweet victory! It comes so seldom.

Head for California

Full Steam Ahead

I graduated from AF Color Photography Processing School and we headed for California. In a small town in Nevada, on good old Rt 40 (West), as we headed out of the town a sign greeted us saying "**Warning next 80 miles NO water - No gas - No Services**" which gave us some pause. It was mid morning and already in the 80's despite being late March. I suspect we got about 10 miles out and the temperature gauge is all the way over to HOT HOT! I turned back to town and went to a service station (*it was also a repair garage in those days*). We get a radiator flush on their recommendation and a new thermostat. "That will surely fix it." I'm told. We start off again and we got about 10 miles out of town and the temperature gauge was all the way over to SUPER HOT! I turned back to town and go back to the same service station. This time they suggest a back-flush! We start off again and at about 10 miles out of town the temperature gauge is at Nuclear Meltdown! I turned back to town and return to our favorite service station that I feel like I now "own" the first pump island and one garage stall. This time they suggest timing the engine! If this is starting to sound a little repetitious rest assured I ain't coming back. For the forth time we start off from this little friggin town. We got about 10 miles out of town and the temperature gauge needle is all the way over, … again! I refuse to go back.

Besides cursing, I think I said some choice stupid thing like "Let the friggin engine blow up I ain't going back!"

Well we drove 15 – 25 - 35 – miles and the poor car is steaming, (*Yeah, remember this is the same car I built a fire under the engine so as I think back now it's a wonder there was any wiring that had insulation on it that wasn't burned off.*) Okay, so I stop the car out in the middle of nowhere to let her cool. There apparently had been a rare rain storm that morning and off the side of the road down an embankment was a small pool of alkali water, the color of skim milk. Melanie said she had never seen a rattlesnake in the "wild" before so while we waited for the car to cool off we decided to go see if we could find her a rattlesnake. So two idiot children go wandering off into the desert looking for rattlesnakes. (*NOTE: We did this stunt with no water, no compass, no map, left no note at the car, no hats - aaaaahhhh!*) Fortunately, I happen to have a great sense of direction and we found the road again and lucky went the right direction to return to the car. (*Note: we did not find a rattlesnake -thank you God- nor did we see another car on highway US 40. Remember this is 1959.*)

By the time we returned, the car had cooled off so I could open the radiator cap. The only container we had that we could carry the alkali water was a lovely wedding present. It was a chrome electric percolator coffee pot. Melanie or I (*I think we switched-off back and forth*) would run down the embankment dip the alkali water from the pool pour it in the radiator, then repeat the process. In the amount of time it took to fill the radiator, the alkali water literally ate the chrome off the coffee pot. I started the car. We went about 10 miles and the heat started rising again, then, … all of a sudden it dropped - way down into the comfort zone. At first I thought, *'well, … I finally broke the gauge'* but no, she ran cool. When I got to the next town and got gas and had them check to see if I needed water. The attendant said "Your full, it looks like chocolate milk, … but your full." After that trip the ol' Blue Bolt never had another problem with over heating and strangely she suddenly was able to go into reverse too. (*I never drained the alkali water from the radiator. I bet it shined like a new silver dollar inside that engine!*)

When we arrived in California I drove immediately to the Photo Lab. Ted ran up to Melanie and grabbed her, picked her up and spun her around in a welcome hug. Melanie had never been hugged by a "colored man" before and quite frankly, at first, she was a bit taken back by it all. It took about 30 seconds with Ted and they were instant "best of friends" just like I was. Sgt Merrill Myers made arrangements for us to stay at her place (*off base in San Rafael*).

First Sgt Obey called me to come up to the Headquarters and said "Okay, I ask all the new married troupes this, "Did you get it doggy style on you wedding night?" I smiled and blushed as I answered "Sure!" Then he asked, "Did you get it Semi-Doggy style?" That threw me and I asked, "What's that?" falling into the trap. He gave a big grin and said "That's when you don't lick it afterward! Congratulations on your marriage, … now get back to work!"

I had a weeks leave and Johnny Brunner (*Who's father was the head electrician at Alcatraz Federal Prison*) took a one week leave as well. He inviting Melanie and I to spend the full week actually living on the prison island with him and his father in their quarters. Of course we accepted. What an opportunity. Just how many people do you know have actually lived on Alcatraz when it was a Federal Prison? Johnny's father had an apartment in the large building adjacent to the arrival dock. In looking at the map of Alcatraz today I would say it was Building 64. From the balcony of Johnny's apartment we could watch the prisoners unload their water drums and their food stuffs (*there was no water supply on Alcatraz, it all had to come in by 55 Gal drums*). Every man had a guard on him with a high powered rifle and was constantly in the cross-hairs of the rifle's scope. If he was going to pass somewhere that the guard no longer have him in his sites he was passed to another guard and they would exchange the prisoners that they had a bead on.

One evening we were in the recreation room playing cards with Johnny and his Dad when a guard rush in and started shouting "Their running, … their running!" and left as fast as he entered. Everyone got up and headed out the door, including Johnny and his father. "Come on!", he said. Melanie and I figured there was a mass jail break, but what the heck, we'll go watch, … this could be historical! All the guards and staff were down at the dock with poles that had gig lines on them and as fast as they would throw a line in the water and jerk it out would come a 20+ lb Black Sea Bass. There was more fish laying on the dock than the whole prison could eat at several sittings.

I can legitimately say that I have served "time" on Alcatraz when it was a prison and not a lot of folks (*alive*) can say that. We were "guests" when the famous "Bird-man of Alcatraz" was there. [*Sidebar. When Johnny got out of the Air Force he became a SF Police Officer and worked his way up through the ranks to become a Precinct Captain. In fact, his actual office was used in the TV series "Dark Knight." which pissed him off quite royally as he had to vacate his office for a couple days every time they came to town to shoot and they would leave everything messed up when they left.]*

The guys all loved Melanie and we would party at every available opportunity. One such evening we returned (*sloshed to the gills*) to Sergeant Merrill Myers home sporting a cheep plastic trophy for winning 'First Place' in a Polka Dance Contest. I have no idea how to dance the Polka, but Melanie did. (*She did it with her Dad and Brothers so I guess she muddled through with me.*) So actually it was SHE that won and I apparently was loose enough in an alcohol induced state to pass for dancing.

I wasn't to stay much longer at Hamilton. I got orders that a new Base was being activated in Oregon in Klamath Falls called Kingsley AFB. I was to be assigned as a Base Photographer. It sounded wonderful, but I was going to miss all my wonderful friends! I soon discovered, that is the worst part of being in the service. You develop such strong bonds with folks and despite promises to keep in touch, the years pass away and you lose contact. It would be so great to find them all again and have a whale of a reunion.

Klamath Falls, Oregon

It was a dewy 5:45am gray dawn outside the Wagon Wheel Restaurant, situated on the main drag running through Klamath Falls, Oregon. There was only one person on the street that morning. We were the only car on the street as we slowly cruised along taking in our new town. We saw him step through the misty morning gray like someone out of the "Twilight Zone." He was wearing a cowboy hat, buckskin coat and pants, cowboy boots, sporting a long white beard with matching stringy hair that would make any hippie proud. He was wearing two six guns hanging low, ready for the draw.

Melanie's stuttered comment is something like, "Ohhh my God, he hee got gu guns on! Get me out of here! Take me home!"

The man's name was Rattlesnake Pete, the K-Falls town character. He had been around during some of the actual Indian wars and had been used as an adviser on several "cowboy" movies shot in the local area. One popular story that allegedly took place in the Wagon Wheel Restaurant, (*which sported a large chandelier in the form of a Wagon Wheel*) told of Rattlesnake Pete and some tourists exchanging words. The tourist challenged the authenticity of Rattlesnake Pete's guns. With that Rattlesnake Pete whipped them out and shot the chandelier off the ceiling. The tourist purportedly paid the full cost to repair and return the chandelier to its former condition. (*I have no way of knowing if that is a true story but it was widely told about town.*)

When I arrived "on Base" it could hardly be called a base. It was only to be a squadron and the highest ranking guy the day I arrived was a T/Sgt Soon we had some officers but I don't think I ever saw anything higher than a Major on "Base." The folks that made "decisions" to send people to set up a base really screwed up on Kingsley, at least as far as the Photo Lab went. They assigned 5 photographers to the base that didn't have a Base Photo Lab. They constructed instead a beautiful new Base Hobby Shop that contained a wood working shop, a car repair shop, a pottery/ceramics shop, leather working and a photo dark-room and that is where we were assigned to work. There was absolutely nothing to do. We would kill for an assignment. All we really did was play cards, chess, or work in one of the hobby shops craft areas.

Then one job came up and I got it! (*Lottery winner!*) It was to shoot aerials of the new Capehart Project to be used in a report to Congress of the US. WOW. I am sure you have heard of the helicopter the Piasecki H-21 Shawnee/Workhorse or known most commonly as the "flying banana."

It has a cargo door in the side and I was given a wide (*very substantial*) leather belt that was attached to a ¾ of an inch in diameter .nylon rope. The other end was firmly attached to the opposite side of the chopper – adjacent to the cargo door. I was to sit at the cargo door, legs hanging out (*as the fellow-not me this time-in the picture is doing*) and the rope adjusted so I could lean out and hold me in just the right angle to be able to shoot a vertical (*down*) shot. I had a little time to practice with it before take off and became fully confident in its ability to hold me. They also had a back up safety line that went around me so I was really covered. I had a radio intercom to the Pilot and basically it was my show, he was just my driver. We were flying a grid pattern above the Capehart Project when he went too far off the center line and I said, "We'll have to go back around on that pass!"

My bad. He does a quick bank left and all of a sudden I lift off the floor of the chopper and am dangling in space. As I later had time to realize what was going on I was perfectly safe, but at that moment all I knew was I was NOT in contact with gravity nor was I touching anything that resembled stability. My instinct said '*grab hold of the cargo door frame!*' My brain flashed '*but you got this brand new 4x5 super speed Graphic camera in your hands*' and then my instinct said '***Screw the camera grab the friggin cargo door frame now you bloomin idiot!***' (*Note: sometime these two - the brain/vs/instinct do not get along nor have a lot of respect for one another*) The chopper leveled out, the crew Chief has pulled me back up to my sitting position but is laughing and as we pass back over the spot I was to shoot the pilot ask, "Did you get it?"

"Ahhh, … no, but we can go back to the base." I said.

"We can go back around again." He said. The Crew Chief laughed all the louder. I was glad he wasn't on an open mic.

"No Sir, we can just go back now." I left it at that. He complied and we returned to the flight-line. I went straight to my NCOIC at the hobby shop and put my new camera case on his desk.

He said "What's this?"

"Open it?" I gestured pointing at the case.

He does, "Where's your camera?"

"Out at the Capehart Project" I respond in a manner of fact manner.

"I wasn't aware you were going to land out there." he said.

"We didn't" I responded.

"Then why... Ohh, …" He dropped his head in his hands and said, "Okay, do you want to tell me about it?"

After telling my story we made a ground trip in search of the camera. I knew approximately where we were and within half an hour we found it. Well, we found the squished remains of a (*former*) beautiful 4x5 Super Speed Graphic that fell about 300 feet onto a concrete walkway from a house patio to an outdoor incinerator (*Again remember this was 1959 they did silly things like open burning then!*)

Melanie and I lived downtown in a hotel that had been converted to apartments. From our window on the 8th story we could see Mt. Shasta in

California. It was a tiny place but it was fine for us and we even had the guys come up from Hamilton AFB Photo Lab to spend an occasional weekend. There was Ted Curry, Johnny Brunner, Stewart Blum, and new guy that came to the lab just as I was leaving, I forget his name. We would go to Lava Beds National Park (*just over the line in California*) and wander around exploring lava tubes. In those days you went to the Ranger Station, checked out lanterns, told them what lava tubes you intended to go down and you were on your own. We actually were in one that we went so deep we came to a place it had markings "Reached this point National Geological Society July 17th 1908 and there was left a empty package (*green label*) of Lucky Strikes. We had to go farther and scratched on the walls, Reached the point farther than those wimps in 1908 the USAF Photographers of Hamilton AFB and Kingsley AFB June (*what-ever)* 1959) and we each scratched our names

We five photographers at Kingsley always pulled "alert" duty at home making sure to call the Air Police as to our whereabouts. Nothing ever happen but we were always prepared with a camera, flash unit (*strobe now*) and plenty of loaded film holders plus a changing bag (*a portable darkroom*) and additional film in the event additional film were ever needed. This was all in a hard fiber camera case about 1 x 1 x 3 foot. One late evening about 12:30 Melanie and I are already in bed when the Air Police call to say they need the Alert Photographer to shoot pictures of an accident. I am told to come to the Air Police Headquarters desk, right inside the main gate. I scramble to get dressed in my fatigues/brogans, grab my camera case and rush out the door, jump into the Blue Bolt and speed off through K-Falls empty streets. Speed is the operative word. I was definitely speeding through town – probably 70 in a 35 mph zone. Soon there were red lights flashing behind me.(*This was in the days before blue lights were also employed on police vehicles!*) Upps! I pulled over, jumped out of the car and flashed my Alert Photographer Chow Pass (*lets you go through the chow hall at any hour of the day or night*) and said panting, "I am the Alert Photographer at Kingsley AFB and the Air Police have called me in for an accident."

"Okay!" The officer said, "Follow me!" And I had a lights and siren 80 mph escort to the main gate to the Base. As we got to the Base gate the police car pulled off out of the way and the Air Policeman in duty waved me through. It was less than a couple hundred feet to the Air Police Headquarters and I pulled my car up front, grabbed my case and ran in. Panting I go to the desk saying, "Airman Voris, the Alert Photographer reporting." The Sergeant at the desk yawns and casually said "Get yourself a cup of coffee, we'll go out in a little while."

WHAT! I glance out the window and the K-Falls Police car is still sitting at the main gate with his lights flashing. He is expecting and waiting to see some kind of action. Flames, smoke, explosions, eruptions of some manner, mayhem, pandemonium, chaos, riots, something, … I'm sure of it. So I pace, 5 minutes, 10 minutes, I have a cup of coffee, 20 minutes. The cop leaves but I just know he is gonna get ME! If not today, … someday! Finally a half hour later an Air Policeman Sergeant said to me "Okay, let's go do this." About time!

We drive a typical blue AF pickup off Base, out across the countryside ,I would say about some ten miles from town. We were in farm country and traveling along some irrigation canals and the Sergeant had his search light focused in the canal. Then we came upon a car half submerged in the canal, its windows rolled up. We stopped, the Sergeant had a hand spot light and shining his light on it called out, "You still in there?"

There was a long pause and then an obviously drunken voice responded, "Yyeeaaasss!"

"Well, get your sorry drunk ass out of there and get up here, cause I'm not coming in after you! And you can't open the door with the windows shut! Roll down the window first" The Sergeant said then turns to me and adds "Just shoot a picture of him as he gets out of the car and be sure you can see his face."

Now I realize that an inebriated individual has antifreeze in their body and a higher tolerance to cold, and I do not know how long this individual had been left in the water but if he went in the water say fifteen minutes before I got the call from the Air Police say 12:15am and he left the water at approximately 2:15am that is at least 2 hours in 45 degree canal water. To add insult to injury, when he finally made it up to the bank, the Sergeant had him ride in the back of the truck back to the base saying, "You're not getting my seats wet." (*At least it wasn't an open bed truck!*)

I was assigned to go on a dignitary flight to Crater Lake area to see the new AF Recreation Area and the AF Capehart Project. There was the Mayor, and City Fathers, Police Chief, Fire Chief, Judges, Sheriff, everyone that was anyone in K-Falls Oregon. The big Chopper was full and fact too full to let me go. I just shot pictures of everyone departing. As the helicopter cleared the top of the peek at the rim of Crater Lake the engine cut out. Now this is not a great thing but not a disaster on a helicopter, because you can free wheel the blades and come down to a safe landing, just not at the location you may have intended. The pilot has called in an emergency and is searching for a clearing to free-wheel into when all of a sudden the blades freeze. Now this is a condition that the helicopter can no longer maintain flight status. It is on the down hill slope of the mountain and just above treetop when this catastrophic event happens. The chopper falls on a tree top that passes it to the next tree top, that gently passed it to the next etc., etc. until the chopper came rolling down to the bottom of the mountain totally in tact and not one major injury. A true miracle indeed. Except for some bumps and bruises and a few cuts and scrapes no one was seriously hurt. If I had been permitted to go, there was no seat for me and I would have undoubtedly been thrown from the aircraft's open door. Everyone else was securely buckled in, including the crew chief which accounts for the fact there were no deaths. I did get to go to the site after all, to shoot the accident scene.

As I said, there was nothing to do generally but play cards and chess so we had tournaments and fancy charts on the wall indicating our individual standings in the Pinochle, Hearts, 500 Rummy, Cribbage, Canasta, and Chess (*I think that about covered it.*) It was a fancy chart, but being a Military base we couldn't come right out and label things exactly what they were so we made it "look" like a production chart – just for the boredom and fun of it. Well, there was a "surprise" IG (*Inspector General*) inspection on the base. (*Note: Inspector Generals are not necessarily Generals, in fact they are seldom actually Generals in rank but they can write up a section and give you much grief if you are below AF standards!*) When the Captain came into our Hobby Shop for inspection the first thing that caught his eye was our "Production Charts" all over the office walls. He complimented the NCOIC and observed that the photographers had to work under extreme conditions yet this was the most organized section he had been to. He thought it should be made a model for the Base. We all just looked at each other dumbfounded, thanked the Captain and slowly slipped the playing cards we were holding our hands into our pockets.

As the saying goes, all good things must come to an end. I received orders that I was going over-seas. I didn't have enough rank to have the government ship Melanie so it looked like Melanie was going to go back to Ohio while I am to go to Wheelus AFB, Tripoli, Libya,. To make this move we decided to build a trailer. Since I worked in the hobby shop I could do it there while (*ha!*) working. I picked up an old trailer bed wheels for just about nothing and Melanie and I started building.

It was the Taj Mahal of Trailers (*well – minus the reflecting pond*) Actually it was more like … Little Abner Outhouse but it was designed to carry all our worldly possessions to date back to Ohio. We even got paint to match the Blue Bolt. The Day came to roll it out of the hobby shop and hook her up to the Blue Bolt. You have heard of the guy that built a boat in his basement and had no way to get it out? My trailer was taller than all the exits of the hobby shop! As I am standing next to the door pondering the height of my trailer to the height of the door one of my friends (*HA!!!*) shoots a picture of me scratching my head. It must have been a slow news day in K-Falls that day because it made front page, a four column wide picture with a headline. "Remember the guy that built a boat in his basement..."

Of course Melanie has to go down to the store and buy lots of copies of the paper and while she is in line the guy behind her is laughing and said to her pointing at the story, "Can you believe that anyone would be so stupid to do that?" Melanie just nods and responds, "Yes,..." gives a big sigh, "He is my husband. She said the guy about died and apologized all over the place. She just laughed. As to the solution to my dilemma? I had to unbolt the part I had built from the trailer base and separate the two. Take them outside individually and bolt them back together. The trailer made the trip fantastic and sat in my parents yard for years as a storage shed.

But for me, I was off to Tripoli, Libya, Africa and Wheelus AFB, I jokingly told friends and family I would be photographing the "sex life of the sand flea." As for Melanie, she was soon to discover she was pregnant with our first child.

Tripoli, Libya -Wheelus AFB

There I was, a 20 year old, stepping out of a MATS (*Military Air Transport Service*) aircraft onto the hot tarmac of Wheelus AFB, 1:30am local time on July 8th 1959 (*I think it was about then.*) I have my total worldly possessions in a duffel bag slung over my shoulder heading for a bus. I am dropped at the 7272nd Squadron orderly room where, after signing in, I am escorted to a barracks and a second floor room across from the Squadron HQ. The CQ flips on the room light and points to a cot. In the room is another individual who has been rudely awaken. He is T/Sgt Clyde Parker. A name that will standout as the most detested man in the Photo Lab history, but I have no idea who he is, what his rank is, or even where he works. It is even a cruel joke that I as an A/2c was put in his room. Anyway, I apologize for the commotion, and make as little noise as possible and throw only a sheet on the mattress strip to my skivvies, turn out the light and hit the sack after my very long day.

The next morning the grumbling Sergeant is complaining about how I disturbed his sleep and he will see about getting me moved out. This is hilarious to me because almost immediately after the lights were out he was snoring so loud I was having trouble sleeping, despite how tired I was. I prayed he could get me placed somewhere else. I report in to the Photo Lab and discover he is there, the second in charge. But you won't believe this! The NCOIC M/Sgt Blotner asks me "Where are you from Airman Voris?"

I respond, "Springfield, Ohio, Sir!"

"Really! That's amazing. What's your fathers name?"

"Robert Milton Voris."

He just shakes his head and grins. "I went through school with your Dad. We played football in High School. I was pals with him and his brothers Emil, and Gordon."

I told him how Emil was instrumental in getting me into photography and about George Wisler. Would you believe it, he also knew George too! Did I have it made or what! It proved to be very important insulation in my protection from Sgt Parker. I soon found out that everyone in the photo lab was under some form of disciplinary action or another brought on my good ol' Sgt Parker. So I knew I had to be careful and watch my normal flippant attitude.

I had only been at Wheelus two days when at close to 2:00am the door to Sgt Parker's (*and my*) room burst open, the light flips on and a shouting voice announces "Damn it Voris, get up! We got partying to do!"

Through the fog of interupted sleep I can barely make out the figure at the door. My god, it is Dunnick, from Tyndall AFB, Florida. At first I think it's a dream, then Sgt Parker gets involved and yells at Dunnick to "Get the fuck out of my room!" then I know it's really a nightmare. I jump out of bed and steer Earl out of the room, turning the light off on the way out as Earl is saying stuff like "What's your problem asshole! I'm here to see my buddy I ain't seen in a long time – asshole!" All the while I'm trying to hush him up!

Once I get him down the hall out of earshot I discover he has been assigned to Wheelus. "Oh shit Earl! That is the Assistant NCOIC you just called asshole! How in the hell did you know I was here and where I was bunking?"

"When I signed in I saw your name and saw the barracks and room number so I thought I'd drop in." He said.

"What time did you arrive in base?" I asked.

"We got in about 8:30 and I have been at the Airman's Club, if you couldn't tell."

So that was A/1c Earl Dunnick's introduction to T/Sgt Parker. They never really got along, but then, nobody got along with Sgt Parker. Very soon after that incident I was assigned to a room with two other fellows that were in the 7272nd Squadron but not in the Photo Lab. They were (*hold on to your hat*) Airman's Norris and Morris. So our room was Norris, Morris and Voris. Now say that fast with a mouth full of crackers!

I should announce about here that I got word that Melanie is pregnant with our first child. Apparently we accomplished this task in K-Falls, but were not aware of it. If we had, I might have been able to change my assignment to a stateside base. Who knows what a different life that would have been.

There was a WWII American aircraft discovered out in the Libyan desert by a British oil exploration team in Nov of 1958. It was generally ignored until the first ground recover trip to the crash site on May 26, 1959. Later some flights were made to the site and I was fortunate to be on one of the early ones. General Spicer, then the Commander of USAFE went down and in his investigation climbed in the tail gunner position, pulled back the bolt and the machine guns fired even after sitting out there all those 20 + years. I get to claim some of the pictures that are at the USAF Museum Wright-Patterson AFB Dayton, Ohio are mine. Time and tide have passed and I couldn't tell you which ones now. There were other photographers too Airman's Pippin, Upp, Spanginberg, Williams, Dunnick and Sgt Arnart (*I suppose even Sgt Parker – ugg!*) If you want to read some interesting stories about the "Lady" and what happen to aircraft's that took parts off of her, read the article in: wikipedia .org/wiki/Lady_Be_Good_(*aircraft*) Better yet. go to the Air force Museum at Wright-Patterson AFB and see for yourself.

I am not sure of the chronology of this, but I guess it doesn't really matter. The road to the Photo Lab was lined with tall date palms. Very prolific, highly prolific I should say. But the base had no harvesting of them, or a cleanup system in place for that matter. As the dates would mature they would drop and drop and drop until we had a driveway that was a gooey, sweet mess of rotting dates. Sgt Blotner said to Sgt Arnart (*the next highest ranking Sergeant after Sgt Parker*) to have all unassigned Airmen go out and "clean up that mess!" Dunnick and I were at the moment unassigned so we were out shoveling the shit. Along with two others that I think was Williams and Pippin. It really was a mess, and everyone was tracking the goo in with it on their shoes and you would slip and slide on the smooth tile floor. But, that was alright though, … because, so far, Sgt Parker was the only one that had slipped and taken a nasty spill. (*tee -hee*)

Anyway back outside, Earl and I run across a batch of fresh, relatively clean dates. Earl sez, "You know, … you can make some good shit out of this stuff if you ferment it."

"Do you know how to do that?" I foolishly ask.

"Well, … all you have to do is add some water, some yeast, some sugar and let it do its thing." Earl said. "Lets do it. I'll get the yeast and sugar at the Commissary at lunch time." (*He had the car!)* So, we squirreled away one 55 gal barrel and filled the barrel almost to the top with the cleanest dates. We dragged the barrel to the boiler room (*it had an outside entrance and only contained - prior to our invasion – the large hot water boiler*) and capped off the barrel with water. Later we returned to drop in a couple cakes of bread yeast and ten lbs of sugar and lock up the boiler room. (*I now know, many years later, that there was absolutely no need to add sugar as the natural sugar in the dates were more that adequate.*)

The street was cleaned to everyone's pleasure and no more tracking in. Time passed and Earl and I totally forgot about our "project." Then one morning there is a strange odor in the lab. Everyone's making sour faces and wondering what died. All of a sudden it struck Earl and me at the same time. Our "project" could be the culprit. We ambled outside (*so as not to appear as if we knew the cause*) and went to the boiler room. Whee-yoo! It was **us** all right. Our "brew" was bubbling like Mauna_Loa during an eruption. But this was black stuff! The smell was the greenish moldy stuff that had grown across the floor and up the boiler to burn at the boilers pilot light and burners. I looked it Earl and said something like, "I think we really screwed up! We created a monster"

"No, no" he said, "It worked! We got to get some big containers and clean this up."

Immediately adjacent to the Photo Lab building was a canvas Quonset hut. It was used to store our excess supplies and seldom accessed equipment. From it we retrieved two empty glass 5 gal carboys. Using a hose Earl siphoned out of the 55 gal drum 2 full 5 gal carboys of something that resembled the color of tar, but plain old road tar would be more appetizing. I kept telling Earl he was crazy and that there was no way I was ever going to drink that shit. He said just wait! In the Quonset hut we put the carboys up on an obscure top shelf way in the back. Again time passed, a long time and again forgot about it.

Then one day on a general clean up one of the young troupes is up on a ladder and said to Dunnick, "What's this stuff?"

"What stuff?" Dunnick said.

"This clear stuff with some black crap in the bottom in the big bottles?"

Dunnick clambers over three rows of boxes and rushes up the ladder in anticipation. His eyes are sparkling. “Jim, Jim,” he calls, “Come here quick! Look! It's done!”

I came over, and saw that the top 7/8th of the carboy is crystal clear and the bottom is a pure black tar looking sediment. We carefully, ever so carefully, so as not to disturb the sediment, brought the carboys down from the shelve. The airman that discovered it still has no frigging idea what we are talking about, but is participating. Earl then is very careful to siphon off the top 3/4th of both into two newly washed carboys. So we now have about 7 ½ Gallons of this crystal liquid. Up to this point it has never been tasted. It is now time to find out if the nearly a year wait has been worth it. Earl poured two cups, one for me, one for him.

I say “You first, if you go blind then I will lead you around.” He takes a cautious sip, his eyes get big and he takes a big gulp and smiled as he said, “Jeez, Jim you won't freeking believe it, it is delicious!”

I took the tip of my tongue test first, wow! He was right. Sweet and as we discovered after 3 or 4 drinking glasses, very potent, and it knocked you on your ass! Oh yeah, ... the Airman that found it? (*I'm not sure of this, but I think it was Kilkenny.*) We made him swear to silence but let him have some. He liked it too. It was a party favorite for the “select few” for a long time. Many profound earthshaking philosophical pronouncements and theological insights were made then. The world would surely be a better place today had they been written down.

Joseph Kilkenny

Still in Tripoli, Libya, Wheelus AFB, but this one individual deserves his own chapter. Actually, he deserves his own book, but we'll narrow it down to a few select incidents and keep it to a chapter. (*I hope*)

What can I say about Joe? He came to us from Dover AFB, which is (*if you knew anything about the AF then*) a secret ridden AF Base. At first we considered he was really an undercover agent. We reasoned that no one could actually be such a physical milquetoast personality, as clumsy, inept, uncoordinated and totally lacking any common sense as Joe presented himself. As it turns out, I am reasonably sure he wasn't a secret agent!

Case #1. Joe arrived and immediately purchased (*on time payments*) from the Base PX a beautiful new Lambretta Motor Scooter. We asked him how long had he driven motor scooters. (*This question was prompted by the fact he pushed the new purchase the 6 blocks from the PX to the photo lab*) He proudly announced this was his first but he had always wanted one. As all newbee's get the Alert Photographer job Joe was of course on Alert for that night. Seems he was gingerly polishing his new scooter when the Air Police came by to announce they needed a photographer to shoot a couple shots on the other side of the base of a B&E (*Breaking & Entering*) He asked the A P if it would be alright for him to follow in his scooter and that way he could leave as soon as he shot his pictures. The A P certainly didn't care, it meant he wouldn't have to transport the photographer back to the photo lab so he agreed.

Well, … according to the accident report the A P filled out he said, "I observed from the start the driver of the scooter appeared to lack even basic operation of his vehicle. As we came around the end of the base road (*that skirts the sea and is at the end of the runway*) he went totally out of control. He went off the road, down the road embankment, across the ditch, up the other side, across the field and ran into the only light post in the whole field – head on. He wasn't wearing a helmet and was knocked unconscious. I immediately contacted the Base Hospital and they dispatched an ambulance, but he was up and walking around by the time they arrived. They took him in for observation. I contacted the Photo Lab NCOIC to get the required photos of the B&E as well as the Scooter accident. I would estimate the scooter at a total loss!" Sergeant Blotner did NOT appreciate our new troupe right from the get-go, but with Sgt Blotner, everyone gets a second chance.

I guess I can somewhat relate to a similar story of my own experience with two wheeled motorized conveyances. Mine was a motor bike. I was working for George Wisler and riding the bus all the time was a drag. A young fellow on my street had a motor bike (*now this was an actual bicycle, with a gas engine mounted on it that drove a belt that gave you a form of propulsion.*) It would be classified today as a "hybrid" and I think in those days you didn't even need a license for it, at least I don't recall having one. It could go about 40 MPH on a flat surface, given a long enough time to get up to speed and coming down a hill you could go 60 MPH, or even faster (*depending on how steep the hill was and how stupid/reckless you were*). But, quite often if it was much of a hill to climb, it needed a peddle assist going up. To the best of my recollection I bought this treasure for $50.00 but right off the bat it had engine trouble. Couldn't keep it running. I tried to take it back to the guy I bought it from but he just laughed at me and said he had the same problem and it was now my problem. Never really liked that guy. I never was much for working on anything that had "oil" in it, but I tore it down and cleaned it all up till it shined like a new penny. Amazingly it all went back together and ran like a top. I had her up and running good for about a week and was just beginning to get confident in the operation when it happen. The street I was on was a long sloping downgrade that joined a main thoroughfare in a "Y" formation. At the bottom of the sloping grade was a STOP sign for my street. I could see if there was any traffic to the left for a great distance on the main thoroughfare as I approached the intersection. Since I was turning right, and there was no traffic to the left and I wanted as much momentum as possible for an upcoming hill ahead on the thoroughfare, I didn't slow down for the STOP. I think (*conservatively*) I went through the STOP banking over at about a 45 degree angle going about 40 MPH. As I get about two/thirds through this fast turn, I am looking directly across the street at a Police Car sitting there. Ohh shit! I instinctively slam on the brakes, which was the wrong thing to do! Both wheels of the bike instantly flip out from under me. I slam down on the pavement skidding down the street, me one direction and the bike another. I can't get up, and the bike is laying in the street, but still running. The cop pulls his lights flashing squad car to the center of the street blocking any oncoming traffic from running over me and slowly exits the vehicle. He sunders over to me and asks how to shut the bike off. I say, just stand it up and throttle it back to off. As he attempts to stand it up, he inadvertently gives power to the hand throttle. The motor accelerates, he stands fast and lifts the front. That makes the bike stand up on it's back tire and he is waltzing my bike around in the street. The gas cap comes off and gas is splashing all over him. Finally he figures out how the hand throttle works and shuts off the motor. Once that beast is under control he comes over to me. I insist I am not seriously hurt and have refused the emergency squad. He assists me, limping, to the curb. As I sat there, the officer admonished me for my careless act and how dangerous it was to do such a thing. He said I "already paid a price and hopefully learned my lesson more than issuing a citation would serve." (*Those were the days when justice was handled directly in the street and not cluttering up the courts*). But I am actually hurt. I can't let on though because I was so stupid. Lucky, again no broken bones, just ripped and torn cartilages in the leg. I spent a couple weeks all wrapped up. I sold the bike for $35.00 as I recall and good riddance. (*Note: It seems age does not improve wisdom as in 1996 I purchased a Honda 250 Motor Scooter. (about 40 years later come to think of it) To make a long story short, I was helicopter air lifted on a Care Flight from Pine Island to the Cape Coral Hospital. The next time you see a football player writhing in pain with a ripped hamstring, believe me, they are not faking it.*)

But back to Joe...

Case #2. I am not too sure you can really hold this one against Joe, but it speaks to Joe's luck. Because he lost his scooter (*and still paying for it*) Joe was feeling he needed something in his life to make him feel, … needed (?) Well, anyway someone was leaving and convinced Joe that owning a horse was a great thing. This was on a Thursday. There were folks out at the horse barns that looked after your horse and you could go out and ride your steed any time you were off duty. When you were Alert Photographer you had the day off during the week. Joe figured that would be great. The deal was struck and he bought a horse. As I said this was Thursday night. Joe was on Alert Friday so that meant he had Saturday off. Saturday morning Joe was preparing to head out to the horse barns an F-100 was taking off, lost power. The pilot ejected and the aircraft came down on the horse barn and kills one and only one horse. Boy you're smart, how did you figure that out? Poor Joe, never even got to clean up his horse stall!

Case #3. I don't believe it ever gets below 50 degrees in Tripoli, but I will say when that wind comes in off the Mediterranean in the winter it feels very cold. You need a blanket if you are on the alert bed. Now the Alert bed in the Photo Lab has not just one blanket but four blankets. (*Why there were four I have no idea.*) The Photo Lab also had a strange oil furnace in the finishing room that operated manually. You controlled the input of oil allowed to enter the fire pan. In the years that I was there we NEVER turned on the oil heater. First there never was an occasion to need it and second it required constant attention. The heater sat about 4 feet from the wall and was connected by a copper 3/8" tubing that supplied the oil, The smoke went up a simple smoke stack made of connecting 4 inch diameter by 3 foot sections to the ceiling that in the finishing room was at least 20 feet. This was a very flimsy smoke stack and on many occasions our "horsing around" in the finishing room nearly knocked it down. But we didn't and it stood those many years.

Enter Joe Kilkenny. Its a cool night, Okay I'll even go so far an say it was cold. Joe decided he needed to light the furnace. The Alert room is one room away from the finishing room and the Alert bed was on the far side of that room. That means in reality the furnace would take a couple days to change of temperature to where Joe was sleeping. But he didn't consider that, obviously. He turned on the oil by cranking the valve all the way open and let the oil pool in the bottom of the fire pot. Taking a wad of paper he ignited he tossed it in and once he saw it was burning he shut the furnace door - and went to bed. He then proceeded to bundle up in two blankets and went to asleep.

For all intents and purposes this should be the last story about Joe Kilkenny. I was the first one in the Photo Lab the next morning. When I arrived I unlocked the front door and was greeted by thick black smoke bellowing out the front door. Immediately inside everything was coated with a black sooty greasy film and the floor was like an ice skating rink. From the finishing room I could hear BOOM – WUSCHH! - BOOM – WUSCHH! I rushed as fast as I could on the slick floor to the room to see what was going on. The oil furnace was tethered by its copper oil line, but bouncing around in an angry arc with each BOOM and belch black oily smoke with each WUSCHH! Apparently at some point the smoke stack came loose during the explosions and all the smoke was now contained inside the photo lab. (*By the way, a photo lab prides itself on cleanliness.*) Now when the stack fell it must have made a considerable amount of noise. The explosions were certainly making a lot of noise.

I rushed to the furnace and shut off the oil line. Within a minute the explosions stopped and I was rushing about opening up windows. By this time the Fire Dept had observed smoke coming from our building and arrived at the same time as Sgt Blotner and Sgt Parker. We find Joe in the alert bed face up, still asleep with the blanket up tight to his neck. His face is as black as the rest of the photo lab and his nose actually had little cones like volcano's and his teeth were black. We can't imagine what his lungs must look like. “JOE!” Sgt Blotner shouts “What the hell happen here?”

Joe wakes up and looks around. Shook his head, coughed a couple times and said "something must have happen with the furnace."

We were all standing outside the Photo Lab and the Fire Chief gave the all clear to re-enter the building but shook his head saying "What a mess to clean up!" Joe, assuming the customary day off after pulling Alert started to leave and Sgt Blotner grabbed him by the scruff of the neck and said, "Where do you think you're going young man?"

"I was on alert last night." He said matter-of-factually.

"Son, you may never get another day off the rest of your days in the Air Force!" Sgt Blotner said. When I left Wheelus (*about a year and a half after this incident.*) you could still occasionally reach into a seldom accessed spot and come out with black oily sooty stuff on your hands. That stuff went everywhere!

As a follow up to this, some fans were stored on a shelf and were coated with the black soot. Joe was instructed to clean them up to look "like new." I was running the Desk and I heard a distraught scream "Oh my God!" and Sgt Arnart came zooming by and zipped into the NCOIC office. Then he and Sgt Blotner and Sgt Parker came out and went back to the Chem Mix area. I had to see what the hub-bub is so I followed.

There was Joe diligently washing the electric fans dunked in the deep sink filled with water. After a great string of expletives deleted (and questions to Joe's heritage), it was determined that if any fan failed to operate at 100% efficiency (*and it didn't matter if it worked before or not*) Joe would be Courts Marshaled. (*Well as it turned out the guys in Camera repair felt sorry for Joe and soaked the fans in a 55 Gal drum of Carbon-tetrachloride and worked on the fans to make them all work fine.*)

Case #4. I was running the desk one day when the Fire Chief came in and said he needed a photographer. All the photographers were out on assignments – except Joe Kilkenny. Joe developed a reputation and no body wanted him as a photographer. The Fire Chief was aware of Joe's reputation but said, "It's a simple job. I just need a couple shots of some open junction boxes at the Airman's club." He pauses a moment then, "Okay, … I guess I can take Joe!" he conceded. I called Joe and he was so excited, and they were soon out the door.(*He hadn't had a job in weeks*)

It was but minutes later and everyone was back from their assignments. An Army photographer and friend Rick Korth happened in and said "Lets go up to the Airman's Club and have a cup of coffee."

Since everyone was back I said, "Sure, I could use a break." So there we were sitting in the Airman's Club and not 20 feet from us CRASH – through the ceiling comes Joe Kilkenny. He lands on his feet holding a smashed 4x5 camera, staggers a few feet in a circle and then falls down. Rick and I run to him and look up through the hole in the ceiling. There we can see the Fire Chief looking down in total dismay just shaking his head. The amazing thing again is #1. Where Joe came through he landed in the isle between tables that had tables set on top of tables. That means table legs pointing up to be impaled upon. #2. He went between rafters, it would have been a <u>nut cracker</u> to straddle a rafter.

According to the Fire Chief this is what happen. The pitch on the Airman's Club roof is very shallow with only a corrugated metal roofing.

They had taken off one panel and were only up about half way to the peak which was less than 3 feet from the roof to the ceiling tile below. The ceiling of the Airman's Club consisted of acoustical tile stapled to 2x4's. The wiring had a junction box without a cover. I (*the fire chief*) told Joe Kilkenny to "kneel down with me" as I wanted to show him what I needed a picture of. As we both bent down I pointed "See that junction box? That is what I want a picture of." All of a sudden he shouts "Yes Sir!" and jumped! Joe walked with a limp for a few weeks but otherwise recovered.

Case #5. We were paid in Military Script, not real US money. We were issued paper 5¢, 10¢, 25¢, 50¢, $1, $5, $10 and $20. It was printed on poor quality paper and not made to stand up to the rigors that the good old green back is subjected to. We had just been paid and Joe forgot that he put his pay in his swim suit pocket and decided to go swimming. By the time he discovered it the money was a wad of pulp. It was his total pay and I felt sorry for him. I suggested that he very carefully soak the wad in our Pakosol (*a solution we use to soften fiber paper and make glossy prints*) and try to carefully peel the wad apart. So Joe did just that. Successfully I might add. As he would free one of the bills from the wad he would carefully place the bill on the photo print dryer where it would go around the heated highly polished chrome drum and drop out in the tray like a brand new just printed bill. Joe was just about finished when Mr. Dehiem of the OSI (*Office of Special Investigation – the Air Force equivalent of the FBI-CIA-NSA-USDA-BSA*) came in to get some photostats made. (*this was before xerox machines – you made photostats of things*) I can't help myself. I have to say as a joke "I hate to tell on a fellow member of my department, but just take a gander at what's going on back there in the finishing room." and point in that direction. Mr. Dehiem looks at me then leans back so he can see into the finishing room. All of a sudden his expression changed and he took off in a dead run. I am in quick step behind to see what happens. To Mr. Dehiem, he see's new Military script falling off a printing press and he grabs poor Joe and threw him across the finishing table, had an arm lock on him and was getting him cuffed before I can say Jack! I as quick as I can, I explain what happen and Mr. Dehiem slowly releases his grip. He carefully examines the money and realizes it has been "laundered" (*that's a joke!*) and finally saw the humor of it. Joe never did quite get it, ... but he was slow to those things.

I really could go on and on about Joe and have often wondered what became of him. If ever there was an individual with a personality trait you could say was "outstanding" I would have to give it to Joe. It would be his unique gift and innate ability to fail at, or screw up, everything he ever attempted. Yet, somehow he was able to live through these experiences that mere mortals would parish. Humm, … maybe he really was a secret agent?

Tripoli & Wheelus

My stories and memories with Mr. Dehiem of the OSI are beyond the ordinary. He seemed to take a special liking to me, if guys of that occupation have any emotions. One advice he would say to me every time he would bring a confession in to the Photo Lab to photostat, "Anybody that signs anything is stupid. If you could get by in your life without ever signing your name you would be better off. It is only used against you NEVER for you." I would say "What about a check?" and he would counter, "See, they are going to take the money away from you and you agree to it by your signature!"

I had a partner in an off base photography business, Paul E Johnson. He worked in the Base Chapel as a Chaplin Assistant. We did weddings and Portraits. In fact we just finished doing all the base dependent school pictures and received our pay the day before. A total of $2,400 was divided between Paul and I. Mr. Dehiem came into the Photo Lab and asked me to come up to the O S I Office.

In the interrogation room I am asked, if I know Paul Johnson. "Yes. Of course, you know why." I tell him. He asked me if I knew how

Paul could get $1,200.?

I answer, "Of course, the same way I did and you know why. I shot your daughter's school picture, remember? We were just paid for the dependent school job yesterday, $2,400. Why are you asking me this?"

"Well, the Chapel was robbed of $1,200 last night and Paul deposited $1,200 in the American Express this morning. But you explained it all. So if you will just write up a statement all will be fine."

"No!" I said, "I will not write a statement!"

"What? Well that is very suspicious. Maybe we better take another look at this and you."

"You go right ahead Mr. Dehiem, you told me a million times to never sign anything. You know I will tell you what ever you want to know, but I won't sign anything!" I was looking him right in the eye.

He looked at me dead pan then with a wide grin said, "Get out of here!" I think that was the real start of our bond!

Another time I was running the desk and Mr. Dehiem came in with a big box filled with pornographic pictures. He said he needed copies for a Courts Martial and while I was at it make him a copy and myself a copy. "What? Not for me!" I said. "And you are going to fry some guy for having all this stuff and then you tell me I can have a copy and you are going to have a copy?" He just looked at me and grinned saying, "He isn't being Courts Marshaled for having this material, it is just goes to establish character. I am happy that we have established yours. You can cancel my copies too."

I was on Alert and Mr. Dehiem came in to the Photo Lab and said "Good, its you.", and then gave me specific instructions as to what equipment and camera and film and lens I was to have. This was very unusual. He had an unmarked car and never said a word as we went off base to a Sergeant's private quarters in Tripoli. There I was instructed to sit on the couch in the living room while the Sergeant and his wife were talking in low tones in the kitchen. At one point the wife left the kitchen and passed me going into the adjoining bedroom. Shortly after, Mr. Dehiem told me to set up the camera on a tripod at this height, indicating about 18" and once I did that he said focus on his hand, which he held at about 16" from the front of the lens. Then he said for me to compute my exposure for a color shot with the flash held at about "here" and demonstrated where he wanted the flash. Again this was all very unusual. Once this was all accomplished he went into the kitchen then into the bedroom and back to me telling me to bring my setup. We entered the bedroom and the wife was sitting at the end of the bed in a housecoat. He told me to set my camera down in front of her but it was too low, I thought.

"Okay Ma'am." He said and she opened her house coat and laid back on the bed spreading her legs wide exposing the unbelievable. "Shoot that!" Mr. Dehiem said as a matter of fact pointing to her genitalia.

I was in my George Wisler mode and did not react, honest! (*seen one seen them all – okay so I have seen a few but not so many!*) Anyway, I checked the focus, got the shot, *(no backup this time to save embarrassment)* packed it up and was out of there with the minimal of humiliation to the lady and the

Sergeant. On the way back to the Base Mr. Dehiem explained. One of the Sergeant's young troupe was drunk and came by their house and attacked his wife. He tried to perform cunnilingus on her. He had a stubble beard and we were attempting to show the rash caused by his beard on her inner thighs in the struggle. I told Mr. Dehiem he should have told me what the mission was because different lighting and IR would have done a better job. He said he was very happy with the way I handled myself in the situation and in the future he would confide in me if he thought it would help the mission.

The Proper Way to Screw Up

Because I was the only one in the photo lab with an altitude and ejection seat card, (*from Hamilton*) every photo assignment that involved a jet ride I got to go on. The Base wanted a Phone Book Cover shot on a 4x5 color transparency with the century aircraft (*F-100, F-101, F- 102, F-105)* lined up in step formation with Leptis Magna *(a Roman Ruins outside Tripoli) -note: I don't recall the F-104 or F-106 was flying out of USAFE-Wheelus at that time*) in the background. That meant we must be in a high orbit point. I had radio contact with all aircraft but it was a dance. My F-100 had to either speed up/slow down, get higher, lower, get closer, get farther away, even if everyone else was in perfect alignment. Basically it was a choreographers nightmare. I shot some shots I knew were too far away but the alignment was perfect. When we tried to fill the frame of a 4x5 it was a mess of misalignment. We finally ran out of film (*and fuel*) and went back to Wheelus. I processed the film and looked at my crap. The full frame stuff was worthless. Then the phone rang and it was the Information Services office. "Airman Voris." the Capt. announced, "I really screwed up. That was suppose to be shot 35mm not 4x5. Is there anything you can do to salvage this or do we have to go back and re-shoot it?" I happen to have a 35mm mount frame sitting on the light table with the pictures. I picked it up and placed it on the ones that were properly aligned with the Roman Ruins in the background. The cropping was fantastic!

"I think I can figure out a way to make it work with what we shot Sir. I will need a little time. Can you give me an hour?" I said to him.

"Just an hour? Wow! Great!" He was ecstatic. He came down to the photo lab an hour later. I destroyed all the bad ones, (*never show your bad stuff*) and trimmed the good 4x5 shots to mount into 35mm frames and made a slide show for him. He was very pleased, took the slides up to HQ to show the Base Commander who in turn called in the unit commanders who all loved the pictures because they could make out the insignia on their aircraft. The phone book was a popular one.

A sidebar story to this is Wheelus supported an aircraft firing range far out in the desert where the pilots honed their skills shooting at different targets using a wide variety of weapons systems. (*There are a couple stories associated with this later.*) The Photo Mission I was on to shoot the Phone Book had nothing to do with the other F-100 we were launching with in tandem. Two Aircraft launch (*take off*) at the same time, one slightly in the lead and once sufficient airspeed is reached the lead aircraft (*on our left*) peels off left and the trailing aircraft peels off to the right to get separation. (*I guess*) At launch we were literally only yards apart as the trailing F-100. Later, while I am still shooting the phone book cover, the aircraft **we** took off with had trouble when it returned to base with its right landing gear. (*The side we were on and slightly behind at take off*) They had foamed down the runway and Earl Dunnick was filming the landing from the back of an open bed pick-up truck. The truck bed had a heavy duty metal framework that bridged the rear of the truck and down the sides so that Earl could stand up and brace himself against it as he shot the movie of the landing.

The driver had positioned the truck 3/4's of the way down the runway and about 25 yards off the edge. That position gave Earl an excellent vantage point. But, the driver kept the engine running and had a safety line on Earl "just in case" it was necessary to "get out of there in a hurry!" The film Earl shot showed the F-100 make a good approach, it flared out great, and it touched down on the two working landing gears (*nose and left*) perfect. All of a sudden the pilot panicked and tried to give it full power to take off. He pulled up at too steep of an angle and the aircraft, lacking sufficient airspeed, slammed down braking off the nose gear and the left landing gear as well as puncturing the fuel tanks. There was a huge fire ball as the remaining fuel in the aircraft ignited. The truck driver of the vehicle Earl is on saw this in his rear view mirror and slammed on the accelerator. In the processed film we saw this fire ball coming toward the camera, then you saw the ground as the force of the truck acceleration forced the camera (*firmly attached to Earls hand*) extend to arms length, then it whipped back and you can saw this wide eyed Earl Dunnick in a frantic attempt to hold on and try to (*occasionally*) shoot movies in the direction of the F-100 chasing them. This bounced around for a good half minute in film and half of it was various (*fuzzy*) strained expression of Earl doing his darnedest holding on and trying to point the movie camera toward the aircraft that was still chasing them. Everyone in the photo lab laughed hysterically in reviewing the film. Sgt Blotner said one thing that that Earl needed credit for. At least Earl never took his finger off the movie camera trigger.

Earl remarked to me later, "It was stuck!"

I had my first supersonic flight over the Libyan desert to film the simulated release of a nuclear weapon from an F-105. Aircraft were returning from supersonic practice missions with damage to the underside of the airframe when a (*simulated*) weapon was released. The theory was it bounced along the underbelly after release, which isn't a good thing.

From my aircraft I had a Bolex movie camera with top speed of 125 frames per second. We were flying so close that all I had in the visual frame was from the weapon tip to the F-105 tail. I gave the count down to drop. I started the motion picture camera on 1 and they were to drop on 0." So 5-4-3-2-1 (*I start my camera*) 0 (*they drop*) It's gone so back to base and process the film. In one frame it's there and in the next frame <u>it's no where in the frame.</u> Gone completely, not even a ghostly image, vanished totally past the tail of the F-105. They ended up having to do this test back in the USA at Edwards with the boys from magic mountain. They had the really fast motion pictures cameras with 100,000 frames per second. Well, ... at least I got a ride in a F-105 going faster than the speed of sound, albeit a short trip.

Another incident with an F-105 involves one that shot itself down out on the El Uotia (*pronounced El Whaa Tea Ya*) gunnery and bombing range that is about 350 miles south of Tripoli in the deep Sahara Desert. The scenario went like this. A series of targets were set up on the ground and pilots are to shoot at them. If an aircraft happens to be at the wrong angle of attack the bullets he fires can ricochet up and strafe the bottom of his plane. In other words if the angle of incidence equals angle of ricochet- bingo! He shoots himself down. This is what happened to the F-105 and why I was out in the desert shooting pictures of pieces. Let me explain what happens on a aircraft crash investigation. First priority to the site is the Flying Safety Officer, second priority is the Photographer to record the site, third is the Base Commander and then Unit Commanders on down the line. We went to the desert crash site in two choppers from Wheelus and in a visual flyover I could see I had a hell of a big grid to shoot. (*Note: The grid meant you walked a pattern of so many feet, took a picture, moved so many feet, took a picture, etc. until the total crash site is photographed*) The wreckage was spread across a wide swath of the desert. I was deep into my shooting when the Flying Safety Officer came over to ask me about how much longer my shooting would take. I said I wasn't even half done. The FSO agreed it was a large site and said that they were going to go back to El Uotia and be back shortly to pick me up. I said “fine” and went back to my shooting. The two choppers took off and there I was alone, in the desert. Just me and my camera, clicking away, walk, click, change the film, walk click. Etc etc, etc. I finally finish the grid, packed everything up and looked around. I am still alone, in the Sahara desert, with a whole bunch of broken parts of a F-105 scattered all about me. They “forgot me” was my first thought. No, they didn't forget me, because they didn't forget about the crash if nothing else. Did you know that the desert is very very hot in the day? Did you also know that after the sun sets it gets cool really fast in the desert? I was out there in my 505 short sleeved shirt and short pants with a “Dr Livingston I presume” pith helmet. I found shade beneath a portion of a wing and fuselage but with the sun set there was no longer a heat source. As dark settled in my teeth were chattering cuss words. Far off I could make out a light going back and forth, first going one way then going the opposite. I wondered if it was someone looking for me. I got into my camera bag and got out the strobe pack and flash it a couple times in the directions of the light. It suddenly stopped. I flashed it a couple more times. It started coming my direction. Finally I could make it out. It was a jeep. It rolled up and the FSO jumped out and said "Jesus Airman, I am so sorry. We got back to El Uotia and the Base Commander along with the Unit Commanders needed to get back to Wheelus so they took the first chopper back. When we were ready to come back to get you, the chopper broke down. I got this jeep and headed out to get you. That was over two hours ago." He had a thermos of coffee, a box meal (*cold now of course but I was starved*) and best of all a flight jacket and a blanket. He praised me for using my flash to signal him. We spent that night at El Uotia. It was a remote site so that meant they received double rations. I had steak and eggs for breakfast cooked to your choice. They flew in another chopper to pick us up that morning.

El Uotia had another mission. It was a site to practice "lob bombing." The target consisted of a white circle approximately 100 yards in diameter, another circle at ½ mile, another at one mile, another at 2 miles another at 3 miles from the center of the white circle. The object was to fly in low over the target, go vertical (*straight up*) and with the center of the target lined up in the pilots rear view sites, release the practice bomb. Then the pilot rolls out and gets as far away as possible before the practice bomb falls back down. When the practice bomb is released it is still going up at the speed of the aircraft and continues to do so until gravity overcomes it and it begins to fall to earth. That was the theory behind the delivery of nuclear weapons and lob bombing. At the El Uotia lob bombing site, 4 miles from "ground zero" at the 4 corners of the target area were telephone poles that have a telephone on them. They were connected to the observation tower that "scores" the drops. At each of the 4 telephone sites were two Libyan guards to assure no Bedouin's (*Arab tribe people of the desert*) wandered onto the range. Scenario: The first "lobber" of the day, an F-100, started his run, went vertical, lined up and ready to release his practice bomb. Just as he did he hit CAT (*clear air turbulence*) which caused the aircraft to shutter violently. He knew his shot would go wide but rolls out and proceeds back to base. (*Note: the practice bomb is only a small shotgun shell smoke charge bomb approximately 3 inches in diameter and 14 inches long with 4 metal fins. I am guessing but probably weighs about 8 to 10 lbs Note ones being loaded in photo on a F-105*)

Meanwhile, back on earth, a Libyan Guard is talking on the phone with the tower. The other Guard is fanning the charcoal fire making their strong morning tea called Shaihee. He hears a "WHAP!" and looks up to see his fellow Guard standing there frozen and then falls over, dead. The practice bomb had come down and hit him in the side of the head. It entered his chest cavity, stayed inside his body all the way down even in his upper leg until it burst out his knee. The bomb's fins attached and drug with it the heart, lungs, intestines, kidney, leaving him virtually eviscerated.

The body apparent softened the landing so that the shell did not explode so there was no smoke discharge. The Guard making the tea went crazy and took off running across the desert screaming something about Allah. Of course I am there with the FSO and a Medical Doctor this time. The Doc places a mirror to the victums nose and detects no breath, feels no pulse on the side of his neck that he still has and said, "I pronounce this man dead."

"What gave you the first clue Doc?" I said

He responded tersely "I have to do that." Then he was down on the ground looking at the man and said to me, "Do you realize you can actually see light all the way through this man? Could you get a picture of that?" Sure I could and did.

The Base Commander was being yelled at by some Libyan official because we killed a national. "How many more of our people are you going to kill this way Col?" he said.

Col Griffith just shook his head and said, "Sir, it is our job to kill the enemy and if we had to kill this way we would never, ever get our job done. The human body from above is only about an 16 inches by 8 inches target and dropping a 3 inch bomb from 20,000 feet, we could never hit anyone. Ground zero has never been hit dead center and we have been aiming at it for years. I am terribly sorry Sir, but this is just a awful accident."

I was missing Melanie terribly and the mail was not a great way to maintain a relationship. It seemed we were always "out of sync." I would send a letter responding to something she said in a letter that upset me.

Then her next letter would be about something that would melt my heart and I'd be all gushy and respond to that. Her next letter would be in response to the one I was upset in, so that would go back and forth. It was a series of manic/depressive communications. I decided I needed her to come over even though it would be very expensive. I just had to find a way to earn extra money. I hit on an idea to shoot pictures on Polaroids in the Airman's Club of guys having fun and selling them for a buck each. All I needed to do was buy a Polaroid camera, get lots of film and have a bunch of little folders printed with a cut out frame to put the picture in. Perfect plan, … zero funds. I wrote Melanie and told her my idea and that I needed $250. seed money. She went to my mother who is adamant about it, “Don't send him $250, he'll just blow it!” MY MOTHER! Can you believe it? Well, Melanie worked on her and pleaded promising that her Government Allotment Check will cover it if all else failed, so Mom relents and Melanie wired me $250. I bought the camera, film, went down town Tripoli and got the folders printed and die-cut. A couple nights later I walked into the Airman's Club and went up to a table with a bunch of guys having a good time. I asked them if they would like a picture to remember the night for only a dollar all framed in a nice little folder (*showing them a folder*). To shorten the story, I sold out of film that night. I bought more film the next day, sold out that night. Soon my biggest problem was having a source of Polaroid film. I had bought all film the Base PX had. The first week I was able to send Melanie the $250 plus an additional $250. The money was rolling in, but Melanie couldn't come because she was too pregnant to travel and the baby wasn't due until mid-March. All the letters now were about her method of transport to Tripoli. One popular way to travel was by ocean liner. That was the plan for quite a while until I saw the movie “Night to Remember” about the Titanic and that was that! She was going to fly. In 1960 flying commercial was still in it's infancy and quite an ordeal. It took quite a while to lining up all the tickets to get from Dayton, Ohio to Tripoli, Libya. It was necessary for me to do a lot from my end too. Once it was announced I had a daughter and the prerequisite time to travel with a baby approached we set the date. I had met all the other requirements, that of having reliable transportation (*I had bought a brand new NSU Printz. $950. USD*) had safe adequate off base housing, (*Had a great place, two bed room villa with some other G.I.'s on a farm near the base that had a irrigation tank that was a great swimming pool*), and I had a round trip ticket for my dependent if they should choose to leave. All was set for Melanie and my new baby girl to come to Tripoli.

Enter Warrant Officer Beck! I got a call to come to the Personnel Office in the Headquarters Compound to see Warrant Officer Beck. He announced to me that I was no longer permitted to bring my wife to Libya, even at my own expense. He said there had been too many bad experiences in the past of Airman abandoning their spouses and that the Air Force had changed the policy and was no longer allowing it. I am a good troupe, though very upset, write Melanie and explain what has transpired. She cries on my Mom's shoulder who happened to be a member of the local Republican Party and a personal school chum of our Congressman Clarence J. Brown Jr. who at that moment was Chairman of the Military Subcommittee on Appropriations.

Okay, now we jump back to me, who knew NOTHING about what transpired in the halls of Congress. I am running the Photo Lab Desk, the phone rang, the Captain who is the Aide to the Base Commander said, "Is Airman A/1c Voris on duty today?"

I respond. "Yes, Speaking, how can I help you Sir?"

"The Base Commander would like to see you as soon as possible, regardless of dress. Could you come immediately?" The Captain asked.

Now ask yourself. You have no freaking idea why you have been "requested" to appear in front of the Base Commander. To be told – basically - get your ass here right now we don't care if you're in your skivvies, what do you think? Right! You haven't a clue! But, … you know you did something - awful wrong. You searched your mind as you're running as fast as your fat little legs will take you, but --- no --- not a clue!

I got to the HQ, panting of course, the Captain clicks on the intercom and said "Airman Voris is here Col." and this kindly voice responds back "Send Jim in Captain, and get us a Coke will you?"

You have to pause here. Stop a moment and catch your breath. While I do mine. WHAT! *"Send Jim in - get us a Coke?"* Is this something out of twilight zone? I was led into the office that I had been in many a time to shoot pictures but not like this. The Col came around and sat in a chair opposite me. After we have a sip of Coke (*what I didn't nervously spill*) he asked me how the job was going, how he had seen me shooting Polaroids at the Officers Club (*I was branching out and also covering the NCO club a well*) and how hot it had been lately. I of course agreed with everything. He finally said, "I suppose you're wondering why I invited (*HA*) you up here this afternoon."

"Yes Sir! That has been a concern." I nervously responded.

"Well, it seems that a Member of Congress has instituted a Congressional investigation into why one Airman James Lee Voris can't bring his wife to Libya at his own expense. Do you know why?" He asked.

"Well Sir, I was told that the Air Force changed its policy on permitting lower ranking Airman from bringing their dependents at their own expense, even if they meet all the criteria, which I did."

"Who told you that?" He asked.

"Warrant Officer Beck in Personnel, Sir." I responded.

"Do you have transportation?"

"Yes Sir, … a new NSU Printz."

"Do you have safe convenient off base housing?"

"Yes Sir, ... with 2 other Air Force Families."

"Do you have round-trip fair for your wife if she wanted to leave?"

"Yes Sir, for her as well as my new daughter!"

"Well congratulations. I assure you Jim, you can bring your family over here. Now if you don't mind, I have a letter I would appreciate it if you would sign. It simply states that I have informed you that you may bring your dependent(s) to Libya and you understand that it is at your own expense. I have a deadline to respond back to Congress on this matter and that is why I needed you to rush up here. I hope it wasn't inconvenient. Now if you still decide to bring her over be sure to stop in at the office. I want to meet her." I signed it of course and then was given the bums rush out of his office.

As I was leaving the kindly voice said over the intercom in a much harsher tone "Sent Warrant Officer Beck in here immediately, regardless of dress." As I crossed the Compound I saw him hightailing it toward the Commanders Office. I almost bet he didn't get a Coke!

Melanie comes to Africa

Melanie Flew with our new baby (*Chai Marie Voris*) from Dayton Ohio to New York to Geneva Switzerland to Malta, and on to Tripoli, Libya. When she was in Geneva, Chai cut her first tooth and President Dwight David Eisenhower was there with Khrushchev. Not sure which was the most historical event.

A wide eyed Melanie arrived at the King Idris International Airport, Tripoli, Libya carrying our baby girl. She, who had never traveled before, was now a world traveler, on her own. All the way from the airport, thru town and to the Base she was a constant "what's that," "what's that?"

Camels, donkey carts, bread ovens at the side of the road, open air meat markets, women in Barracan's all were new experiences. She was drinking in everything, with "what's that!" As we rounded the base along the sea the sun was setting. Off in the distance were little fishing boats. Each boat had a lantern on it and Melanie in her constant barrage of "what's that?" pointing at the fishing boats. I said "Tinny Tinies" and she said "Oh!" Now, why I said "Tinny Tinies" I will never know. It makes no sense, no meaning, but I said it and the moment passed. No more is said or thought about it.

The next morning we went to the Personnel Office at the Headquarters Compound. We had to see Warrant Officer Beck to get Melanie's and Chai's visa extended from a couple days as a tourist to a resident. Beck took her passport and half looked up. He said, "Your Visa is extended to 30 days, then you have to leave." He stamps her passport, hands it back and looks at me with an evil grin like "screw you" Airman.

We leave the Personnel Office stunned. Then I remember. The Commander basically ordered me to stop by and bring Melanie in to see him when she arrived. Give it a try. We crossed the Compound and went to the Commanders Office and I introduce Melanie and Chai to the Capt. I mentioned that the Col said he wanted me to bring Melanie by when she arrived. Apparently it was perfect timing, the Col was free and we were ushered right in. After some nice talk I was able to slip it in that she would be required to leave in 30 days."

Why is that?" the Col asked.

"Warrant Officer Beck said her Visa was only good for 30 days and she would have to leave."

"Do you have $2.85?" He said.

"Yes Sir." I responded, but wondering what that was all about?

"Give it to me." He said. I did, he got into his drawer, took Melanie's Passport and applied something like a postage stamp, then marked it with a rubber stamp, initialed it and handed it back to Melanie. "There my dear, you may stay in Libya as long as you wish. The $2.85 is the cost of the Libyan Stamp, a Libyan pound note. Now, go enjoy Libya."

As we left the office this time I heard the definite angry voice on the intercom say "Get Warrant Officer Beck in here right NOW!" I took some pleasure in seeing Mr. Beck running toward the Commanders Office. This time I noticed he was aware that Mr. and Mrs Voris were standing there. I never had a problem from Warrant Officer Beck again.

A few months later Earl Dunnick's wife Regina, came over to Tripoli. The day she arrived Earl happened to be off on assignment so Melanie volunteered to pick her up and show her around. Regina was the same as Melanie, "What's that, what's that?" When she come's to the beach and sees the little fishing boats, she said "Whats that?"

Melanie proudly announces, "Those are Tinny Tinies"

There is a pause and Regina said, "They are WHAT?"

Melanie drops her head, shaking it saying, "He got me again!"

Vice President's Visit

I truly loved my job as an Air Force photographer. I was always doing something different, day after day it was never the same. One day I was out in the desert shooting a plane crash or a dead body hit by a practice bomb. Then the next day I may be flying in a jet fighter shooting aerial pictures of other jet fighters and later that same day I might be covering a fashion show put on by the Officers Wives Club. Occasionally I spent the day covering the special guests that came to our base like Royalty of a host Country or Vice President of the United States.

I was assigned to cover Vice President, Lyndon B. Johnson, when he stopped over in Tripoli on his "Round the World Goodwill Tour" in either late 1961 or early 1962. (*I think this was part of a trip Kennedy sent him on*

to Vietnam and the beginnings of that mess) As a photographer I always tried to be "invisible" and unless I was setting up a shot I'd try to stay in the background to capture the events as they unfold. LBJ, (*and his secret service*) along with the Base Commander Col Griffith (*my buddy*) were in the Base Commanders Office with the Black Prince and his body guards.(*Then the reported to be the operational head of Libya because the King, King Idris, was ill and dieing of Syphilis. [Note this was before Quddafi]*) After a nice chat Col Griffith shows the Prince out, LBJ does his quick slip hand shake and went back and sat down. For a few minuits it's just LBJ, the Secret service agent and me in the Commanders Office. He looks a me and said, "Where are you from son?" I respond proudly, "Springfield Ohio, Sir!" LBJ grumbles to his SS agent (*not looking at me or responding to me.*) "Jesus fucking Christ. Don't they have any God Damn Texan's around here?" Then he looks at me and said "I want a copy of every picture you take today. You make sure they come to my attention." "Yes Sir!" I said. But the ass-hole, the way he talked, I never sent him one picture. It isn't everyone that can say they disobeyed a direct order of the Vice President of the United States.

I was also fortunate enough to be in and out of the big wigs offices many times. If you do your job efficiently and in a professional manner those guys appreciate it. They hated the bungeling photographers that fumbeled with their cameras or had no talent for posing a group or how to get them quickly at ease with a minimum of disruption. Apparently that was my major talent and best asset. Anytime a job came up to go to the big USAFE Commanders office, Brigadier General Spicer, I was always sent if I was available. General Spicer was the Enlisted mans General. He believed in his troupes and annually held a raffle that if you were one of the eight drawn you went on Safari to South Africa with him, all expenses paid, except you had to buy your own ammo. Because I was in and out of his office so many times shooting pictures of him presenting this and that award, he quite often called me by my first name. I was very sad when they decided to move USAFE Headquarters to Ramstein Air Base, in Germany. Shortly after the General left we were "blessed" with the arrival of a new Lt in the Information Services office that drove us photographers bonkers. He must have taken a photo course in college because he figured he knew everything about our jobs. He would go so far as to say where to focus, what "f" stop and shutter speed to use and would pose every shot. (*You can imagine that this did not set well with my style but he was the Lt and you did as you were told.*) We all did our best to avoid jobs that the Lt was going to "run." Then I was assigned to go to the Commanders office with the Lt to shoot the Base Commander receiving the USAFE Year's Outstanding Safety Record Award. General Spicer had flown down from USAFE Headquarters in Germany to make the presentation to his old friend Col Griffith. The Lt and I entered the Commanders office for the picture. The Lt immediately started directing the General and the Col where to stand and started to tell me in his customary style where to focus when General Spicer said, "What are you doing Lt? I think Jim knows a hell of a lot more about this stuff than you do. Why don't you go over there in the corner and watch and learn." My God, the expression on the Lt's face. If he had been slapped, his face wouldn't have been redder. He retreated immediately to the corner like a kid sent to his room without supper. I went into my best professional mode and got them relaxed, a couple good laughs and nice shots of the award presentation and we were out in less than two minutes. The only thing the Lt said to me as he drove me back to the Photo Lab was, "Are you somehow related to the General?"

"No Sir." was all I responded. After that any job I went on with the Lt he never offered me photo tips nor did he pose the subjects. On a couple occasions he would softly mumbled, "Well, I guess you know how to handle - (*this or that*)." I never answered because it wasn't a question.

Col Griffith hated to have his official annual portrait taken. It was called a 36-93 and most officers called them their obituary photograph. But it was required, and because the Col hated having it taken, it inevitably was an awful representation of him. I was shooting a presentation picture in his office and as I was leaving he said, "I have to make an appointment to come down to the Photo Lab and get my 36-93 updated. I don't see why you can't take one of the great shots you take here in the office and use them. You make me look half human here. Those portraits I look like a corpse." I quipped with him and said, "Well the problem is I never had the opportunity to shoot your 36-93. I'd like a chance to see what we could do." I was surprised that he said he was free tomorrow afternoon at 3:00 and asked if that would work. For the Base Commander, you make it work. When I got back to the Photo Lab I talked to M/Sgt Blotner about the Col coming. I made a special request that the Photo Lab be closed for an hour. He ask me why and I said I needed to have the confidence of the Base Commander and if there were other people running around it would break the effect I was trying to get. (*I think he realized I was bull-shitting him big time, but also realized I wanted to do something that gave him plausible deniability if it went bad.*) So nearing the appointed time Col Griffith was to arrive the Photo Lab was cleared out. Air Police were informed that the Alert Photographer was standing by at the Airman's Club. In advance preparation I had all the studio lights set, camera ready, posing bench ready, film ready. The Col arrived alone in his staff car and entered the Photo Lab. I immediately led him to the studio and requested that he take a seat. I then said, "We are going to get some really great shots today Col Griffith."

His response with a bit of a scowl, "Yeah, well, let's just get this over with."

I went to the Finishing room and opened the film refrigerator to recover a bottle of beer, the favorite of the Col (*I had observed what he drank at the Officers Club when I went around shooting my Polaroids.*) I didn't open it, but I set it down in front of him with a church key and said, "There is no one else here so we can get some really great shots once we get relaxed!" First there was a look of shock, then a look somewhat angry that I thought "*Ooh oh I went way over my bounds this time!*"

Then he looked around and said, "We're alone?" I nodded, he said, "You know it is against Air Force regulations to have alcoholic beverages in a duty station?"

"Yes Sir!"

"We are alone?" he said again.

"Yes Sir, and that beer is getting warm." He looked at me and I know that for a split second he thought he should just get up and call the

Air Police to haul my smart ass off to the clink, but he didn't. He took the church key and popped the lid. We got some great portraits that day and it was done on only two beers (*all his - but he said he would pay me back the next time he saw me at the Officers Club*) As I recall he took the empties with him, which I think falls into the category of removal of evidence. I never told anyone that story until well after I knew it could do no harm to the Col.

What Bugs Me

I realize I was living in Africa, but sometimes I forgot that it isn't quite the same as Ohio, Colorado, California or Oregon.

I returned to the photo lab very late from shooting an alert mission. I was dog tired and I had been looking forward to some restful sleep after a long day. I recall that it was a cool night and I just slid into the alert bed (*properly made to military specification – all tucked in*) flipped the lights off and started to drift off. You know it feels when you are really tired, bone tired, and your muscles twitch? Well I started twitching – all over. It started with the sensation on my back and legs. I ignored it at first, thinking I was more exhausted than I had imagined. But soon it became obvious that I couldn't be "that tired" so I decided to get up and investigate. I turned on the lights and pulled the covers down to see if it was just my imagination or if I had "visitors."

OMG & Holly Shit! The bed was full of little tiny baby lizards that the mother had crawled in between the sheets and laid her eggs. Now most had hatched and there were easily 20 of them. Some were squished from me sliding in and the others were apparently trying to bond with their new surrogate mother. I didn't respond well to motherhood. I was jumping around trying to get them off me and the (*imagined*) ones on my back. I had cold chills from that and despite the hour, walked up to my old barracks to take a shower. (*I was living off Base now with Melanie*) I never got into a bed after that without checking to see if there is anything looking for a mother.

If I haven't mentioned it before, most of the time you pull "alert" duty nothing happens and it is very boring. On such a "nothing happening" hot Sunday I decided to take a mid afternoon nap. Unfortunately the Photo Lab had a broad concrete expanse for parking aircraft between it and the sea, some half mile away. That caused the normal North African desert hot air to be heated even more, so what little sea breeze there was, the air was heated beyond the normal "hot." One thing about it though, it was a "dry heat" and all jokes aside about that, you seldom sweat. The perspiration would evaporate instantly. On the Armed Forces Radio they would give the weather and many times the announcer would say something like "The air temperature is 115°F and the humidity is unmeasurable" As a result we were instructed to take salt tablets and drink lots of water regularly. There were salt tablet dispensary machines all over the base and told it was a Courts Martial offense if we collapsed as a result of dehydration. But, I never heard of an actual case of anyone being Courts Martial. But I digress.

Since there was no one was around the lab, I was in just my skivvy undershorts. The bed was pushed up next to the open screened window to garner what little air was moving. I also had a fan going blowing air across my near naked body. It made laying on top of the sheets reasonably comfortable and I soon drifted off. My arms were up to expose my "pits" to the moving air. My head was supported by and resting on my hands, with my fingers interlocked.

At some point in my nap I woke to the strange feeling something on my abdomen, like someone was lightly tickling me. I raised my head to see what it was. There on my belly was a big hairy spider that was easily the size of my hand. Now nothing, I repeat NOTHING, in God's creation scares me like a spider. I would lay down in a pit of snakes rather than touch a spider. My whole body turned to instant sweat. I was terrified and unable to move. Then as he (*Okay I guess I don't know if it was a he or she monster*) started slowly walking across my stomach toward my chest. I really was starting to freak out. Thinking as fast as I could I tried to reason out the situation. I probably didn't want to swat him on me – thinking that it may drive his poison fangs into me, or that my swat may not kill him but just really piss him off. I recalled seeing movies about this sort of thing and they would "brush off" the spider with the side of their hand. My hands were still up, fingers interlocked behind my head so I slowly slid my right hand out. I stealth-fully moved my right arm way out and off to the side of the approaching spider, hand flat to act as a scoop or paddle. As he was approached the nipple line of my chest, I bravely acted. I made a quick sweeping motion to knock him off.

Not quick enough! The sucker jumped and landed center of my face. I will never forget how that felt. It was like a rubber glove filled with warm water and dropped on my face.

"Squish" he landed and I am screaming and swatting my face. I'm up from the bed and running blindly across the alert room sputtering and slapping myself not knowing where he is. In my near naked state I run into the huge copy camera in the alert room that is on rails (like a train) and go ass end over teacup. Injured and bleeding I, still frightened, get up and run from the room.

Half an hour or so later, I have gathered my wits about me and I clean up and bandage my cuts. I found a baseball bat in our sports equipment bag. I decide to re-enter the alert room and face my monster. It was to be a duel to the death.

After two hours of terrified searching, flipping things over with the bat, poking in corners, checking high and low, I couldn't find him. In fact I never saw him again and I looked, believe me I looked, again and again. Every time I had alert and had to sleep there I would check everywhere I thought a monster spider could hide. Many times after this incident I would sit in a chair in another part of the lab to spend the night with my feet propped up on another chair.

Despite the fact it has been over 50 years since this incident, I can still feel that monster landing on my face. There are just some things you never forget!

Rejeb

One of the really great things about living in a foreign country and off base is you become involved with other cultures. You make friends with people of another ideology and ways of life. Enter, Rejeb Ali Tarhunni. First, let me explain the name. What we call the last name is the town they are born in so Rejeb was born in the Village of Tarhunni. The middle name is his Fathers first name, so all of Rejeb's children, boys or girls carry Rejeb as their middle name just as all of Rejeb's brothers and sisters middle names were Ali. I "inherited" Rejeb from my next door neighbor a G.I., Pete Alexander that was rotating back to the US. He advised me of the many "advantages" of having Rejeb as your friend. First of all, Rejeb was very influential in Tripoli. He was the credit Manager of the Bank Of Sicily and was "connected" to many government officials. (*We will discover this in greater detail later.*) The importance of our friendship was realized soon after our introduction. Melanie was taking our Arab Housekeeper home when she came upon a section of road covered with water. (*Yes we could even afford a housekeeper over there. One of the great "perks of foreign living.*) There had been a recent rain and it had flooded the road way. Melanie did not understand that you can't drive across the sandy desert to get around the flooded road and in a short time was bogged down. She looks out and saw a mob of Arabs running at her and she panic's. She jumped out of the car and took off running. Another car had pulled up to the water blocking the road and was in the process of turning around when Melanie ran up, opened the car door, jumped in and started screaming to the driver "Go, go!" All he see's is a mob of Arabs running toward them and he floors it. They are Italians and don't speak a word of English. Melanie can't speak a word of Italian yet she is able to direct them to take her home. She was crying. She figures she has lost the car and really in trouble. I'm concerned for her of course, I tell Pete Alexander, who gets Rejeb to come over. A short time later Rejeb drives up in our car, perfect condition and explains. He talked with the village elder that told him what happened. The villagers saw the lady stuck so they were rushing out to help her. When she was running away they kept yelling for her to come back, they just wanted to help her. It was all just a misunderstanding.

Rejeb, with his Land Rover driver Heidi would take me with them out into the light Sahara Desert to go Gazelle hunting. Sometimes it was just Rejeb and I and sometimes it was with Arabs I never met before. One such time we were with a fellow I didn't know and we had shot about ten Gazelle. We were down in a dune depression dressing them out when all of a sudden we were flanked by members of the Libyan Army (*well armed I might add*) all along the dune ridge. They had a good bead on the four of us.

(Note: Prior to this moment I did not know that it was illegal to hunt Gazelle in Libya!) Rejeb and this other Arab didn't look the least bit concerned, put down their knives, wiped their hands and walked up the dune to the officer in-charge of the unit. Heidi and I stood there as targets for the Libyan Solders to have something to shoot at. They were too far away to hear and since they were speaking in Arabic I guess I wouldn't matter if I did. I watched the Officer in charge of the army bow and give a gesture, (*that's usually a good sign*) he blew his whistle and in seconds the Army is gone. Rejeb and the stranger came back and we finish dressing out the illegal Gazelle. Later I got Rejeb off to the side and ask what happen with the Army Officer. He just shrugged his shoulder and said "I just introduced the Army Lieutenant to my friend. In your country he is what you call a Justice of the Supreme Court."

I was alone with Rejeb on a trip not really that far from Tripoli, maybe 75 miles south. The land was dry and flat as a billiard table. We were driving at about 70 mph when all of a sudden Rejeb starts jerking the wheel first one way then the next. This was before seat belts so I was sliding my ass all over the place. Finally as I desperately held on shout, "Rejeb, what the hell are you doing?"

"Old mine field." he said without a care in the world.

"WHAT! That is Bull Shit Rejeb!" I said. (*Wrong thing to say!*)

Rejeb slams on the brakes. "It is what?"

I repeat, "That is bull shit, we couldn't be going through a old mind field and if we were you wouldn't know where they were, not ever single one." That is when I learned to #1: believe Rejeb when it came to anything in the desert and #2: Never challenge him, you'll lose. He just looked at me and grabbed his shotgun, opened the driver side door, stood on the step and pointed off to the side of the vehicle. He fired and about 35 yards away Boom, there was a ground explosion that I assume was a mine. He cocked and pointed ahead and about 20 yards – Boom. Then across the hood about 40 yards – Boom. He fired another direction but it didn't explode. He said it must have been a dud mine. He got back in the Land Rover, hung the shotgun back up on the rack, restarted the vehicle and not saying a word zooms off again zigzagging for a while. I desperately wanted to ask, "But Rejeb, what if you forget just one?" but I didn't dare.

On this same trip Rejeb had ask me to stop by the Base Commissary and get a case of 24 Morton's Salt. They only cost something like 10 cents each. Rejeb was going to pass them out to the desert Bedouins that, to them, salt was gold. It was a overcast night, Rejeb stopped the Land Rover, took a couple salts and walks off into the ink black desert to the side of the vehicle. A couple minutes later he returns and asks me to come and meet his friend. I can hardly see my hand in front of my face and all of a sudden I am aware that Rejeb had disappeared. To my left on the ground was an ever so faint glow emanating from a hole in the ground. I heard Rejeb say "Down here." Kneeling down I became aware it is a ground dwelling and entered through the small hole. I was met by Rejeb and his Bedouin friend who in honor of his guest had fired up some charcoal to make Shaiee, a strong tea. The fascinating thing about his hovel, it was constructed primary from PSP, the portable steel interlocking sheet that were used to make instant runways in WWII. His quarters were about ten feet long, four foot wide and four foot high. It had some little shelves, a tiny cook stove made from scrap metal and a vent smoke stack plus our entry/exit way. The only light was from the tiny fire. As I am making an inventory of all of this, unbeknownst to me, Rejeb donned a rubber, full head, Ubangi mask and was sitting right beside me. I notice the Host had taken notice of Rejeb and as I turned to look at him he made the awfullest sound. I'm not sure, but I think that our new poor Bedouin friend had to move. It's probably is easier to dig a new hole than clean that one up!

On a trip out with Heidi, Rejeb and I we were camped way out in the desert on a moonless cloud covered night sitting around the campfire and the two were arguing in Arabic. (*Kinda leaves me out!*) I broke in and asked what the discussion is about. Rejeb said pointing as he speaks, "Ohh, this stupid man said Tarhunni is that way 134 Kilometers and I say its that way 163 Kilometers." I suggest they make a wager. They did and Rejeb said, "It's my Land Rover so we'll go my direction and if I am off by more than one kilometer I will double your pay, If I am right within one kilometer then I owe you nothing. Fair? (*Geez I figure that is impossible. We are out in the friggin desert, no stars, no moon even, no landmarks to see. My GPS today couldn't do it!*) Heidi eagerly agrees, it's a no brainier as far as he is concerned so Rejeb draws a line in the sand pointing toward his goal and writes 163K. The next morning they spent a half an hour further arguing about the alignment of the Land Rover. Once agreed a compass is set and we started our trek. I am hoping there are no WWII Mine fields in the way. I ask but Rejeb is to involved watching Heidi to make sure he stays dead on course. When we come to a wadi (*A dry river bed*) sometimes these have really steep eroded banks. Go around? Not on your life, that adds kilometers. To make the story a bit shorter, we rolled into the little desert village of Tarhunni as the speedometer clicks over to 163.3 Kilometers at the very edge of the village and 163.5 at the center where the well was. As a matter of honor, Rejeb did not pay Heidi, but he did give Heidi's family food and equivalent reward that would not be considered as payment for work.

One other time we (*Rejeb, Heidi and I*) came to a WWII bunker in the desert and decided to stay the night behind the walls. I thought that was cool. It was near dusk when we pulled in, we hadn't seen anyone or anything all day. We were out pretty far. We had a camp fire, had some Arab food and went to sleep early. It was just barely dawn when Rejeb woke me and he looked worried. If Rejeb was worried, I was worried, I could read the same expression on Heidi's face. Rejeb handed me a shotgun and said "When I tell you I want you to shoot in the air as fast as you can pump out five shots. Then reload and stand by!" I knew not to ask why right now so I wiped the sleep from my eyes and got ready. Rejeb was at the old bunkers walls looking through a port and after about two minutes he said to Heidi and I "NOW!" We both fired our shotguns as fast as we could, I quickly reloaded and stood by. After a few minutes he signaled for me to come over and peep out. What a magnificent site! Sitting on a sand dune not 50 yards from us were three male Tuaregs in their black turbans and black robes holding the old flint lock long rifles. They silently come in the night and the whole clan pitched their black tents just yards away. Rejeb said to fire again, and we did. Then the three Tuareg men stood up, and within 20 minutes they disappeared. I don't mean they went away, they vanished. The reason Rejeb (*and Heidi*) was worried was the Tuaregs this far out in the Sahara still took slaves when they can. Rejeb wanted to show them that our fire power was superior to theirs and it would cost them more than what we were worth. Rejeb never took me that far out again. He said he was friends with all the Bedouin but even he would be cautious in trading with the Tuaregs.

Melanie, Chai & I went to Rejeb's house for dinner on a number of occasions. It was the custom that the men eat together and the women eat separately in another room. Of course the host, Rejeb, sat at the head of the table and the honored guest at his right which I was afforded this place. On many occasions there several Arabs I did not know that could not speak English. (*And of course there was no way I could master the guttural sounds of Arabic language*) Rejeb would, if something was said that everyone laughed at, translate it so I was made somewhat a part of the conversation. During one of these translations a tray was passed that held small peppers and I was gestured to take some. I took one. I noticed they were all eating them by the hand full (*like they were baby carrots*) I was smart and only bit mine in half. (*Stupid, stupid, stupid!*) Mt. Vesuvius in Italy that buried Pompeii was not as hot as this. Everyone at the table was laughing at me as I choked and spit. I was up and dancing around. Rejeb gave me some Shaihee tea and that helped, but I didn't taste anything with my tongue the rest of the meal. It was dead, … well dead would have been better. Tingling like it was laying in a hot frying pan for the evening. I had visions of what eternal burning in Hell must be like. At some point in the evening I needed to go to the bath room and excused myself. When I returned to my seat I noticed my pee-pee was starting to burn, it became more and more uncomfortable until it got downright painful. I was squirming around in my seat until I have a tear in my eye. I reach up and rub my eye and shortly my eye starts burning like my nether-lands. Aaahaa I surmise, it's the juice off the peppers on my fingers being transferred. I am a walking contaminator of fire juice! Needless to say I was the entertainment that night.

As I indicated the women ate separately in the kitchen on the dirt floor (*hard packed and well swept Melanie recalls*). Melanie was about 7 months pregnant the women wanted to check her out. First the were patting her and feeling her arms and breast indicating she was too skinny (*Melanie was always a thin woman*) and then they were patting her belly and wanted to pull up her blouse. They were also chanting with their characteristic Arabic song where they click their tongues rapidly while singing. (*it's shrill and scary to a westerner and Melanie was starting to freak out.*) Melanie was not really into this and shouts "**JIM**!" Rejeb and I come and Rejeb explains to Melanie what is going on. He apparently told the women to cool it - you're scaring the lady and then tells us the women said we are going to have a boy. (*Which we did!*)

One last story about Rejeb. He tells about his life in North Africa during WWII. It seems the Germans under Rommel were willing to pay in gold for any operational British weapons the Arabs could steal. Rejeb said he got pretty good at it and was making good money. It apparently was hurting the Allies war effort enough (*not just Rejeb's part I'm sure,*) but the British also started offering "rewards in gold" for all the German weapons the Arabs could steal. Rejeb said "This was very good lesson in economics, no empty load each direction!"

Meanwhile Back at the Desk

I mentioned that quite often I was put in charge of the assignment desk. This was the primary contact point for everyone coming into the Photo Lab requesting services and also the phone answering point for the Lab. If in 1959-61 you got a phone call from the states it came to you via the overseas operators which were a very convoluted series of transfer hand-offs. So if you intended to call someone you wrote to them first and had it all arranged so that you would be standing by. That said, let me introduce one great guy A/2c James T. Pippin, from Mississippi. He was the only southern boy in a duty section and barrack's filled with Yankees. Even off Base at best he only had British to hang with, so his delightful southern accent became Yankeeized! His mother had made arrangements to call him on his birthday so he was excited waiting for her call to finally come in. I was at the desk, the phone rang, I answered "Base Photo Lab" and a voice said "This is the Rome Overseas Operator, Go ahead London," then I hear "Go ahead New York, and then Go ahead Party," and a voice as sweet as sugarcane in a most southern bell accent and long drawl said, "Isss Airr-maan Pip pin tharr!"

"Yes! He is expecting your call, just a moment!" I shout for Pippin and he comes running. He grabs the phone, "Hello, Mom?"

Again a voice as sweet as sugar and long drawl southern accent said, "Isss Airr-maan Pip pin tharr!" Pippin answers with, "Mom! It's me, James." She said again ignoring his plea, "Mayy Ai speak ta Airr-maan Pip pin tharr!" Pippin answers with, "Mom! It's me, James." She said again Airr-maan Pip pin tharr!" Pippin answers with, "Mom! It's me, James." She said again ignoring his plea, "May Ai speak ta Airr-maan Pip pin Palease!" Now frantic Pippin said "MOM, can't you hear me, It **is** me, your son James." She said, "Look ya damn yankee, I don't know whatcha done witt my boy, but you shore ain't him." and hangs up. Pippin was devastated. He had no idea he had come to talk like a Yankee and for weeks he walked around forcing himself to try and "talk southern."

James Pippin, Bob Kennedy, Dave Huntington, Earl Dunnick, and yours truly decided to celebrate the "Lady Be Good's" anniversary by taking a little 30 mile walk across the desert. It was even semi-officially sanctioned by the Air Force in that the Air Rescue Squadron planned to follow our planned route. There was even a story about our proposed hiking adventure in the base newspaper "The Tripoli Trotter." We were starting off on a Saturday morning. The idea is Regina (*Earls wife*) and Melanie dropped us at a village "well" on a road crossing in the desert. According to our wonderful (*provided*) Air Force aerial maps it is about only 30 air miles from the drop off point to the mountain town of Gharyan that has a hotel and also sported a British outpost. Our wives were to meet us in the hotel in Gharyan on Sunday. Then we drive home. Simple plan, contingent was if we looked like we couldn't make it Sunday the girls were to stay in the hotel and we would be there Monday. We even had the Air Rescue Squadron going to drop us supplies of water and rations for practice if for no other reason. What could possibly go wrong?

We each had two water canteens and a separate two gallon plastic container filled with water, along with our sleeping bag, food supplies, a pistol with ammo and of course camera's. (*Note: I know in retrospect to what our boys in Iraqi and Afghanistan pack on their backs and this trip is a laugh. But remember we were a bunch of Air Force photographer weenie's that carrying the groceries in from the car was a big deal.*) So, filled with confidence we started our trek. We hadn't gone a mile and we came to a little Arab village with a well.

We are warmly greeted and we press on, a mile farther and another village with a well. Then another mile, another village and well. The 2 gal bags we are carrying are very heavy and cumbersome (*A pints a pound the world around - so two gallons is 16 lbs.*) It is obvious we don't need to keep carrying these so we give them to the villagers. We have only gone about three miles but we reason there are probably going to be villages all along our route. After all, the Air Rescue guys are going to drop us water and supplies so why are we beating ourselves up with this extra 16 lbs of dead weight. Makes sense, right? Come on, right? (*This was a group decision!*) It was slowing us down too. We started our "hike" at about 7:00 and it was almost 10:30. We calculated we were making less that a mile an hour. So sixteen pounds lighter, stronger determination to "pick up the pace" we head on out of the little Arab village. That was the last village we ran across. The canteens were soon near empty (*we had no reason to assume we needed to ration the water*) We kept looking for the Air Rescue search plane, but no where in sight. (*Note: The Air Rescue Squadron knew the exact location we started from and the destination we were going to. The total search area was framed by highways that even if we were totally lost we would run into a highway at some boundary point. I don't know to this day how it's possible that they NEVER found us, nor did we see a search aircraft, even on the distant horizon*) That night we were (*guessing*) only about 14 miles from our start point. It was starting to get a rougher going and that slowed us down. The AF Aerial map didn't show the rough terrain (*This was BG -before Google!*) and we soon discovered it was worthless as a ground navigational aid. Again not overly concerned about water yet, we started the next morning and run into a rugged 500 ft ridge that was a bugger to get over. (*It isn't on the map*)

That mountain exhausts us and we all have used up our water. We are back on desert but we can see more ridges ahead. No Air Rescue, no Arab Villages, we trek on. Now it starts to become a problem. We (*foolishly*) decide to split up and search for water. If you find it you're suppose to fire three shots in the air. If you hear it, respond with one shot and head toward the source of the three shots. If you are lost and need directions again fire two shots. I was about ¼ of the way up the ridge following what looked to me an old worn stream bed in the rock and there it was! A small crystal clear pool of water bubbling out from under a bolder to a small (*about 3 foot diameter 2 inches deep*) pool in a rock depression. As the water overflowed the small pool it evaporated as it trickled over the large bolder and exposed to the hot sun.

I would like to say my first function was to fire the pistol three times, indicating I had found water. I didn't let that thought even cross my mind. I was in survival mode, I – had water. I fell face first into the pool and sucked up a big mouthful. It was probably the most wonderful water I have ever had in my life. Cool, sweet, - MINE!

The first thing that happen was my system was obviously dehydrated and the sudden influx of so much water made me sick. I rolled over and threw up. The rational mind would have said "wait a second, sip a little don't gulp it down!" but I wasn't rational. I dove back in, threw up again, and then I started calming down. I began to see what was happening and took pause. I sat there for a few minutes, then I carefully filled my canteens, cautiously sipped the cool water and then and only when I knew I was satisfied and I had MY water, I fired the pistol.

It was a fascinating study of how very close we all are to our most basic survival instincts. I fired my pistol, way off in the distance was a single shot here then another way off another direction and a double shot. I fired three again and the first to arrive was Pippin. He dove in (*like I did and got sick*) Huntington and Dunnick were about neck and neck coming from slightly different directions. Huntington beat Dunnick by seconds but Dunnick pulled him out of the way and it was like a tussle over this small pool. They all did the same thing, took in too much, threw up and did it again. Then trailing in was Kennedy. We all observed this same response at finding the water despite our trying to persuade him to go slow at first. The poor little pool was having a hard time keeping up with the demand. I would guess it was a good hour later before everyone was finally back to being a human being again. We all remarked they couldn't believe how we had were acted. We were all best friends and yet that didn't matter at all when it came to survival.

It took us another hour or more to garner the courage to finally leave our little water hole but we knew we couldn't stay there forever. We didn't know it, but we had another one of the friggin ridges to climb over before we would start the climb up the mountain to the city of Gharyan. With renewed spirits and a profound sense of unity in purpose we set out for the last leg of our journey. Once over the ridge we discovered an Arab

One of the three "ridges" we had to climb over

Looking back from the top of our first ridge.

foot path that took us up the mountain to Gharyan. I will admit it was a very rough ordeal for this tenderfoot, but what a triumphant feeling it was to march into Gharyan that late Sunday afternoon. We made it to the hotel's bar where we immediately ordered beers. We were dirty, tired, looked like we were the shot up wounded cast out of some WWII movie, but damn proud of ourselves.

A Brit bloke stopped by our table and quizzed us as to our sojourn. We proudly announced we hiked from such and such wells to Gharyan. He said "What? Bout 30 miles is it? My lads do that before breakfast ever morn-in." Gotdamn Brits!

Paul E. Johnson-Partner

I mentioned before that I had a business partner, Paul E. Johnson, in association with the Mr. Dehiem story. He should have a proper introduction now. Paul has been a major part of my life and entered through a strange door. I was having coffee at the Airman's Club when this guy comes up and boldly said, “Hi, I'm your competition.” I look at him like he's crazy, I have no idea what in the hell he is talking about. Competition? Competition in what? “What are you talking about?” I ask.

“In Photography. I shoot weddings and portraits. I think we should become partners.” he said.

Now I have no knowledge of this guy, he doesn't work in the Photo Lab, He isn't an Army Photographer, he's wearing an Air Force uniform. I have shot all the Base Dependent School portraits and shoot portraits (and weddings) of Officers and Enlisted. What did I need a partner for? I had Melanie. He said, “Why don't you and your wife come over to my place for supper with my wife and son and hear what I have to propose?”

Well, what would it hurt to "see" what my competition was doing? Besides, I knew I wasn't buying what he was selling. I sure didn't need to split the money I was making with someone.

Well, that evening pregnant Melanie, Chai and I met Paul and Ginger (*and their son Mark - the same age as Chai*) at their house in downtown Tripoli.

A nice place, and Paul had a darkroom to die for with all new equipment. He also had several great new cameras that I lusted over. His proposal was, "what I was charging was way too little." He showed me his price list and almost everything on it was nearly 10 times what I was charging. I was shocked and told him there was no way G.I.'s could afford those prices. He cajoled me to giving it a try "just for one month and if I didn't think it was working out we could part company, no problem." Well, reluctantly, ... I agreed. Amazingly we were getting business I never had before. Sure, some drop off at first from the lower ranks (*I just told them to hold on for a little while, I'd get back to them*). But suddenly the higher ranking Officers and more importantly the Oil Executives were having photo work done by us. I couldn't believe it. The Air Force job was always my priority of course, but every spare minute of time off was now being spent in this new company called Chai-Mark Studio (*Chai after my daughter and Mark after*

Paul's son.) We soon had to have larger and more prestigious facilities. That is when we got an adjoining duplex out on the opposite side of Tripoli from the base on the main road. It was on the Mediterranean Sea, walled completely around the house with garages and servant quarters in the rear that we turned into Studios and darkrooms. We had an Arab house boy and a cleaning woman to help Melanie and Ginger. Melanie was about to deliver and Ginger (*Paul's wife*) was about 4 months away from giving birth herself. On August 22, 1961 Victor Mark Voris was born, officially registered as being born in Sukajumma, Libya (*closest Libyan town outside of Wheelus AFB*)

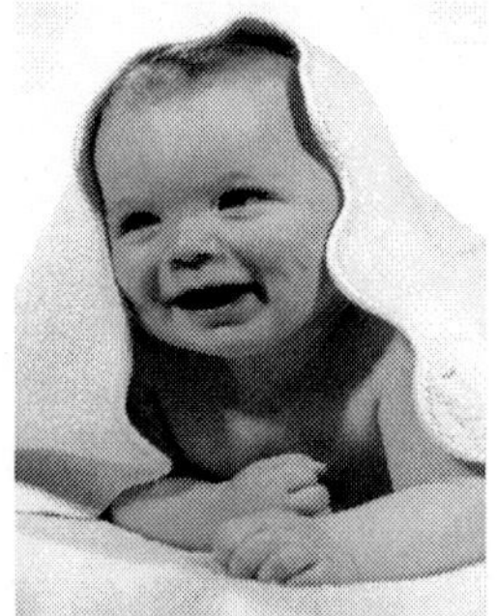

In November that same year Victor died of SID's (*Sudden Infant Death*) and we take the infant's body back to the US for burial in Springfield, Ohio. I was offered an assignment at Wright Patterson AFB in Dayton Ohio, (*right next to my hometown*) but we both wanted to get back to our "home" and friends -and business in Tripoli. As it turned out I reenlisted in

the Air Force there and even signed up for another three year tour in

Tripoli. Can you blame me, we were making very good money for a lowly Airman.) So we got settled in, believing we had another three more years to go in Tripoli.

I was confirming my stories with my old friend Paul Johnson when he commented that he was disappointed I left out the story of our harrowing escape from the old city. I asked him what in the world he was talking about. The following (as far as I am concerned either #1. never happened and it was a dream Paul had. or, #2. It was something trivial (to me) and a joke I was pulling on Paul and so insignificant that I forgot about it (even to this day). But, I promised him I would report it as HE told it, yet I must say I do not recall this misadventure at all. (But- he said he would send me pictures he took that day)

According to Paul, he and I were "exploring" in the old castle in the Old City down at the harbor. It was a museum of sort and he said I apparently got curious and opened a door I wasn't suppose to open. He recalls that I said, "Oh my god, … it's a Harem filled with half naked women! Quick let's get out of here, the Eunuchs are coming after us with big knives."

He said he never ran so hard in his life, he just believed me despite the fact he never saw into the alleged Harem nor did he see any knife welding

Eunuchs. Now, not that I am beyond doing (or saying) such a thing or it is past me to conger up such a joke on Paul, it's just I do not recall ever being in the old city and in such a place. I will have to eat my words if he ends up sending me a picture that proves I was there. If I was, wow, maybe I did look into a Harem filled with half naked women! Damn, where was my camera! (*As of publication date I have not received any pictures from Paul that would back up his story – he said he can't find them!*)

One morning that I had Alert Photographer, Melanie was coming out to the base to pick me up at the Photo Lab. We were suppose to shoot a job (*since I had the day off after pulling alert.*) About a half hour before she was due to arrive the Air Police show up saying they needed the Alert Photographer to go on a job. This was the days before Cell Phones and I had no way to tell her I was going to be tied up for some undetermined length of time. I couldn't even tell anyone at the Photo Lab to tell her because no one had come in yet. I scribbled a note and left it on the door of the Photo Lab. "Tell Melanie had to go on Alert Job - don't know when I'll be back!" (*Everyone knew Melanie*)

The job ended up going down town. Damn, those always ended up taking 3 or 4 hours. We came up on a car and low and behold it's my car!

It's sitting on the sidewalk, and it has one side all scraped up and mangled and the other side is worse. The windshield has written on the inside in red lipstick some numbers. No sign of Melanie. I'm panicking, but I shoot the required pictures and we head to the police station as normal. All the motorcycle police in Tripoli knew me as Mr. Jim. Nearly all of them had trained in the USA in New York's Harlem district. After my being out and about in the local scene for three years and shooting pictures of them on their Harley Hogs, I would drop prints off to them. That's why I was well known as Mr. Jim in the Tripoli Police Department. When the Air Policeman and I entered the Police Headquarters I immediately recognized Melanie's voice coming from one of the interrogation cubicles, "He hit me!" she was insisting. I rushed in and she was shaking but obviously alright physically. "Mr. Jim!" the officers eyes lit up. "Is this your lady?"

"Yes! This is my wife!" I said.

"Tell her a police truck not hit her and everything is okay, good."

Melanie looks at me and stubbornly said, "NO, look on the windshield, I wrote down the police trucks number, they slammed into me and that slammed me into the wall dividing the lanes. I was still in the car when a bunch of people pick the car up and carried it to the sidewalk to get it out of the street. I finally got out of the car when they told me that you would come here at the police station.(*speaking to me*)"

I could see she was angry not hurt. "Melanie, do as the officer said. Just write a statement "*a Police truck did not hit me.*" and sign it." I turned to the officer and said, "Is that what you need?"

"Yes Mr. Jim, that is good, no problem then."

So, reluctantly and grousing all the time, but Melanie filled out the accident report with only that on it and the car was fixed without question by the insurance company. We told our agent the true story and he nodded and said, "I understand."

I have confessed to having done a lot of stupid things in my stories, certainly not to make me out to be any kind of a hero. This incident probably takes the all time winner as being the dumbest stunt I ever pulled. I was downtown Tripoli to shoot a quick job and I left the car window open. When I returned I got in and started to put the key in the ignition, when I noticed a WWII rusty old American type hand grenade sitting on the seat next to me. The pin was missing (*so obviously pulled*) but the handle hadn't popped off. I carefully open my drivers door and got out. This was smart. Had I took off running would have been brilliant! What I DID was reach in and very carefully pick up the hand grenade and gently carry it to a ditch and softly place it on the ground. I retreat to a safe distance. I suddenly think, NO, … no, I can't leave a live hand grenade laying in a ditch for some poor Arab kid to come along and discover. So I go back and gingerly pick up the hand grenade and ever-so carefully place it back in the car where I originally found it. I return to where I was shooting and using their phone call the Base Bomb Squad to come remove it. They came, they did, they took it to the base where it exploded in their pit. I confessed the full story to the guys in the Photo Lab and of course they are going nuts laughing at me at how stupid I am. But that isn't the end of the story. At the next Commanders Call the Squadron Commander Major Aunie calls for me to come up to the stage. I have no idea what this is about. Then, in front of the whole Squadron, he is patting me on the back and proclaims **me** a hero because I did the right thing and called the Bomb Squad when I discovered live ordnance in my vehicle. That moan sound in the audience was coming from my friends and fellow photographers.

We had a lot of wonderful parties at the house on the Mediterranean Sea. We even got a (*its life time had expired*) 20 man life raft from the Air Rescue Squadron and held a party on it. That got a little harry when after a few hours someone said “Where's land?” We had to have several out of the raft on one side kicking to try and push it back to shore. I took us several concerned and harrowing hours to get back to land. For your information, I assure you 20 man life rafts, are NOT navigation-able.

About 6 months into my extension to stay at Tripoli I received orders that I had been selected to be an Instructor at the USAF Photography School at Lowry AFB in Denver, Colorado. While it was a great honor to be selected, I questioned how that fit with my approved extension in Tripoli. They said that the Instructor job took precedence so off we went. At least now I was an E-4 rank over four years so the Military paid for shipping all our household goods as well as shipping Melanie and Chai. Melanie was also pregnant again and was due to deliver in late July. We were moving the first week of July.

Denver, Colorado

Lowry AFB

Wow, I am going to be an Air Force Instructor. Would you believe that when I report in to my new duty station (*the Photo Technical School*) office and met the boss (*a Civilian this time a gentleman named Charley Ridenhour*) he asks me where I was from. "Springfield, Ohio Sir." I respond. "Really, so am I." After some checking, we find out he had dated my mother! Two duty stations in a row and the bosses are tied directly into my parents. What are the odds.

To become an Instructor you had to go to AF Instructor Training School, which was basically a Speaking Course. They wanted to make sure you could stand up in front of a bunch of people and speak with some air of authority. They convinced us that a good Instructor could teach any subject if he had command of his audience and the proper tools to teach with, which were curriculum and training aids. Well I had no problem giving my presentation speeches because as a photographer I was accustomed to being in front of Generals and even the Vice President of the U.S. and directing them. So the course was a slam dunk for me. The next thing I had to do was sit in with an Instructor for a few weeks and "observe." My mentor was A/1c John Spagnolla a short wiry Italian that had just the right mix of devil and angel that we melded together perfect. We were like mustard to a hotdog or butter to bread. It was instant friendship because he was crazy and funny. My very first day with John he said "You will do great if you just follow what I do. Watch and learn!" It was a new class of Airman, <u>their</u> first day, my first time to observe. He told me to go in the classroom first and take a seat in the back. I asked, "What if someone is sitting there?" He looked at me and stared until I said "Oh, yeah, I just tell them to move!" He nods. I go in the class room, the room snaps to attention, I proceed to the back of the room and the seat in the far corner I want is occupied but a seat up front is empty so I tell the Airman to go sit there. He does, I say to the class room, "As you were!" and everyone sits down. About a minute later John entered, the room again snaps to attention, (*I stay seated*) John kicked a chair so that it slide up next to the table at the front of the classroom, leaped up on the chair then onto the table. With his hands at his waist he screamed at the top of his lungs, "**I'm God!**" Then he drops the tone a couple decibels and adds, "And if you don't believe it stay standing at attention and I'll come down and prove it to you. Otherwise, SIT **AT EASE**!" Everyone sat down. I am proud of myself, I was able to contain my laughter.

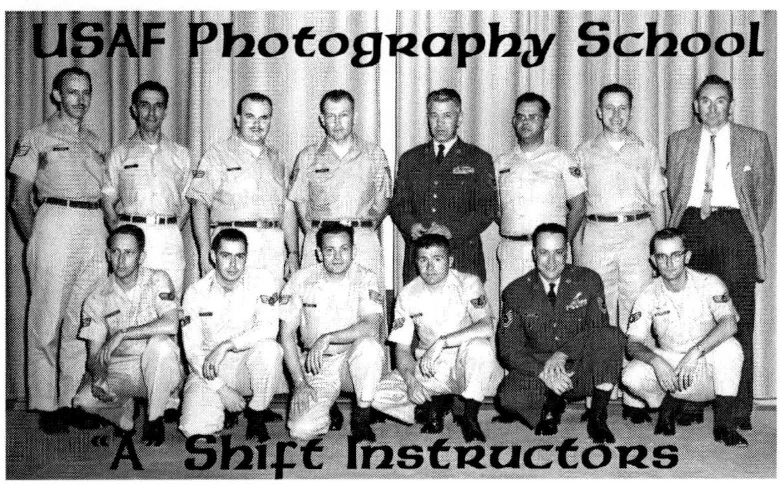

In the picture above John Spagnolla is 1st row second from left and I am standing directly behind him.

I was an "A" shift Instructor, which meant my teaching schedule ran 6:00 to 11:30 and lunch to 12:30 then you had your office duties 12:30 to 2:30. About every month you got "Remedial Training Instructor Duty" which was really a throwback to High School's "Detention" for bad boys and girls. All you did was babysit the troupes that had been "bad" in class for two and one half hours. This was held at 6:30 to 9pm so you could get the "B" shift (*12 to 5:30 p.m.*) bad boys too. Well John Spagnolla and I were at a bar right off base one afternoon (*starting at about 3:15*) and we are drinking beer. At about 6:15pm John happens to mention, "I wonder who has Remedial Training Duty tonight?" It hits me! I DO! Shit.... I am about three sheets to the wind and I only have 15 minutes to get to base and open up the building. I rush out of the bar, make it past the MP at the gate (*Meaning I didn't run over him*) and got to the Remedial Training building about 5 minutes late. They were all gathered outside waiting and can easily see I am snockered. All the other times I had done this duty everyone just came in and sat quietly doing their homework. Previous times I had even ask if anyone had questions and no one ever did. But this time, when all I wanted to do was put my head down on the desk and rest, the dirty little bastards were pestering me with the most mundane and trivial questions. It was definitely a conspiracy because they were lined up coming to the desk. It was the longest two hours of my life! About 10 minutes to 9:00 John comes in wearing civies but with his AF military raincoat and blue hat. He appears sober, and immediately everyone returns to their seat, it's quiet as a church. John and I step outside and I tell him they all have been little bastards but it was my fault. He said "Bull Shit, we'll teach the S.O.B.'s not to mess with an Instructor." So at the appointed stroke of 9 just as they started to get up and leave, John orders them to fall out in formation. Now get this picture. It was dark, John (*and I*) have a flight of recruits (*about 30 I suppose*) standing out on the road. He (*and I*) then proceed to march them back to their barracks. John said it was necessary discipline and I went along with it, so I was culpable too.) We are having then shout cadence at 9:30 at night marching on dark streets without safety gear or road guards out. WE are breaking a BUNCH of safety rules. The next morning apparently everyone of them turned ME (*mostly*) and John in for what we did.

As I am standing tall (*with John beside me*) in front of the Squadron Commander the next afternoon facing these charges. The Commander said, directly to me, "I can understand this behavior from you Airman Voris, but from you Airman Spagnolla, ... I find it unbelievable." What? It's understandable behavior from me? How in the world had I gotten that reputation (*already?*) and my mentor, the guy that put me up to this mess it is unbelievable? Then the Commander said, "I can't have recruits thinking they can get my Instructors in trouble so for now we'll let this pass. But, I never want to have another incident like this again do you understand Airman Voris?" And he didn't even mention John in that.

"Yes Sir. Thank you Sir. I assure you it will never happen again Sir." I said. John and I saluted and we left. I found out that all the little S.O.B.'s that turned us in, ended up on extra KP duty for 21 straight days. It's nice to be King!

To clean our negatives it was customary to use isopropyl alcohol and the School got three 55 Gal barrels of it a year. Either by error, oversight or substitution we were shipped three 55 Gal's of pure grain Medical Alcohol. (*For the uninformed that is 190 proof 95% pure drinkable alcohol*) The Head of the Tech School, Mr. Ridenhour said that there was no way he was going to put medical alcohol out on the floor for students to have access to, so he made an offer to all of the Instructors. He would trade equal volume of his pure grain medical alcohol for isopropyl alcohol. It was a mad scramble by us Instructors to find isopropyl alcohol in Denver. Every pharmacy and grocery store that sold it was cleaned out in short time in an ever widening circle from Lowry AFB. It was like the shock-wave of bomb blast spreading ever outward. That three 55 Gal barrels is the equivalent of 2,640 eight ounce bottles of isopropyl alcohol. Or 1,320 sixteen ounce bottles. Believe me some of us had to go to Golden, Bolder or even to Colorado Springs to find a bottle of isopropyl alcohol. If you used 2⅓ parts distilled water and 1 part medical alcohol it made a nice 80 proof vodka so just one sixteen ounce of medical alcohol gave you 37ounces of 80 proof. So three 16 oz and one 8 oz made you a full gallon of really good stuff!

One day as I am teaching I see the back of the room rise up in the air a few inches and it travels through the room (*practically instantly*) to me. I just experienced another one of those ground wave earthquakes. I still don't understand how solid buildings can so easily flex with those wave earthquakes and not show any obvious damage.

Bright Idea

At a Commanders Call they showed us a classified film on the infrared heat-seeking rocket and how once it locked on the heat signature of an aircraft's exhaust, it was a sure kill. They went on to explain how this heat from the aircraft exhaust radiated out in a conical shape and once the missile was in that cone it had a lock. They mentioned that the "enemy" also had this technology and if anyone had any suggestions on how to counteract it you should send in a suggestion on a standard suggestion form. Well that night I am trying to think what I would do to stop this missile and the idea hits me. The missile is basically using a infrared light-meter sensor to guide the missile. If you blind the sensor, the missile doesn't know where to go. I had just read in a magazine that lasers were the newest thing and I also knew as a photographer a bright light temporarily disabled a standard light-meter. I reasoned then that a laser could blind or burn-out a missile sensor. So in so many words, I said this on a standard AF Suggestion Form and sent it in. Maybe a month passed and I had completely forgotten about the suggestion. I was teaching my class and over the classroom intercom came an announcement, "INSTRUCTOR VORIS, REPORT TO THE OFFICE IMMEDIATELY, PLEASE!" Now, they never interrupt a class unless it is a dire emergency. I can't imagine what it is. Did something happen to Melanie, the kids, my parents, world war three, something I did or didn't do? It all is running through my head. I get to the office and Mr. Ridenhour is holding a phone out for me to take which is not a calming thing.

"Airman Voris." I answer.

"Yes, Airman Voris, this is Col (*I don't remember who*) at SAC Headquarters calling. Will you be at your base tomorrow?"

"Yees Sir?" I say with a drawn out questioned yes.

"We would like for you to be at your flight-line at 09 hundred hours, class A blues to await arrival of a debriefing officer. Can you be there Airman Voris?"

"Yees Sir." I say AGAIN with a drawn out questioning yes. Before I can ask what this is in relation to he disconnects. I told Charley Ridenhour what was said but he has no idea. I went back to class and finish the day. The next morning I was at the flight line. So is the Base Commander and the Military Band and a car that has a flag with 2 stars on it. I am standing alone. A small twin engine prop plane lands and taxis over to us. The Base Commander is out to greet the arrival, the band plays the car comes and picks up the two star General and drives over to where I am. The guy in the back seat motions for me to get in. I do and I am sitting next to the two star General. He introduces himself (*sorry- I do not recall his name*) and he is holding some papers, one of which looks vaguely familiar. His first words after the introduction are, "Tell me more about your idea!"

"Idea? My idea Sir? What idea are you referring to Sir?" Like apparently I ever only had one idea in my life. No, actually I was stalling, hoping for a clue as to why I was sitting there.

"This is your suggestion isn't it?" He pulls out and shows me the AF Suggestion paper I had sent in.

"Ohh, yes, that. Well, until this moment I had no idea why I was being call here to talk with you Sir. That, yes!" So I basically re-explained what I had written down.

"Yes, yes!" He said impatiently, "The laser part works fine, but here is my problem." Using his hands like an aircraft and a finger like a missile. "I have this missile coming in on me at 1,200 mph and we are trying to paint a target the size of a quarter with a beam the diameter the size of a pencil lead. Any suggestions how we might do that son?"

NOTE: This is a major juncture point in my life. I do not realize that at this moment, (*because I'm really stupid*) I could change everything in my life's direction by a few carefully chosen words like, "Well Sir, I have several theories I would like to explore!" or even "Sir, I think I do have a couple ideas that might just be what your looking for, but I would like to test them first." But NO, I said, "No Sir, that is all I have to suggest."

The General just nodded, said to the driver to take him back to his aircraft. When we got there he thanked me for the original suggestion and told the driver to return me to my duty station. I did have the joy of pulling up in front of the Photo School in a car with a two stars flag flying on it.

Paul comes to Denver

Melanie was pregnant (*again*) and her Mother was having fits that she wanted her to come "home" and be under the care of a "real doctor." So sometime in mid-summer of 1963, Melanie and the kids, Chai now 3, and Rob 1, take off to Ohio to stay with Grandma, until the new baby is born. I was in contact with Paul Johnson who was out of the AF now that his tour in Tripoli and enlistment was up. He and his family had returned to his home town in Indianapolis, Indiana. He was struggling along trying to get by with a small photo studio there. I convinced him he should come to Denver and he could stay with me. I had an "empty nest" and Ginger was content for her and the kids to go to Kansas to be with her parents while Paul got settled in Denver. So Paul came and we lived in my 8'x40' trailer (*off Base in Aurora*). I also had another small 8'x24' trailer (*I called Odd-ogg*) that I had stripped out and re-made into a darkroom and finishing room. It had all my beautiful darkroom equipment I brought from Tripoli including two huge 1 inch thick marble slab table tops, Chromega 4x5 color enlarger, Pako print dryer, Pako print washer, and all the tools/accessories to make a real first class professional darkroom. But we needed a studio.

Paul of course has the days off and I am teaching at the base until

2:30 so it is up to Paul to find us a studio we can afford. (*Free is really hard to find!*) We end up with a second floor space but not in the greatest part of Denver. It is a very large space and affordable but conducive to only be a commercial photography business because with an address on the "other side of the tracks" in the upstairs of an old building you don't attract a wealthy portrait and wedding business. But we had to start somewhere on a near zero budget. (*My income from the Air Force*)

We built a darkroom in the space and hooked up my darkroom trailer (*Odd-ogg*) to take it to the new studio. It was way too unbalanced (*not intended for road travel with marble table tops*) and very heavy on the tongue. But, we only had to go a few miles so we figured we could go slow. We were almost there when the trailer hitch broke lose from the car, and the trailer tongue dug into the macadam plowing a 3 inch deep furrow in the street. We were very lucky because we were going along Cherry Creek and if the trailer had decided to veer to the left it would have careened off into the river, losing everything. I was amazed that the police didn't issue a ticket and were most helpful in getting us a tow truck. I think it was only about another mile or so to the studio where it was to be towed to, but that cost us $30.00 as I recall.

We were scraping by with little jobs here and there and Paul comes up with this nonsense idea that we need some models. "Models!" I exclaimed, "For what?" He said that we needed them in our inventory on call for when we had a job that called for models. It would be a selling point for our commercial photography if we had our own models. Like most everything else I relented and went along with his "idea." Paul put a simple ad in the Denver Post that said "Models Wanted - $5.00 hour, call (our phone #)" It only ran for one day and the response was unbelievable. We literally could not hang up the phone for a second before it would ring. Paul decided that we would hold "Auditions" and here was his plan. If you wanted to be a "parts model – hands, feet, face" we paid $3.00 an hr. A full body "underwear/swim suit model" we paid $4.00 an hr., and a partial or full figure nude was $5.00 an hr. Paul made appointments for "test shots" in what ever category that wanted to be a model in. The first time I arrived at the studio after my day of teaching I was met with people lined up on the steps leading up to the studio. Holy crap, what was going on, I wondered. Paul has people filling out applications while he is in shooting a few test shots on what ever category they selected. He is happy to see me as he is running around like a chicken with his head chopped off. It was well after 10 that night by the time we finished the line up The same happened the second and third days with some let up for the following week. In such a short time we have collected a list of hundreds of potential models. Granted some have NO chance of being a model (*We had one old lady in her late 70's that wanted to be a nude model! Paul shot her test shots that way of course. I often wondered if she might have been a great comical calendar girl for the older generation.*) While 50% were less than desirable model material we did have a solid 25% that was outstanding model potential. The funny thing is we never (not once) used a model in any commercial job of ours, but we probably made more income from the models that from the photographic business. What happened was one day shortly after our foray into shooting all the test shots and setting up a filing system, a fellow stopped into the studio. He was the treasurer of a Denver Camera Club and asked if we knew how to obtain models. We told him that we were also a modeling agency and could supply models, depending on what he wanted. He asked if we could get him nude models for a Camera Club Shoot. We said most definitely and showed him our list. He found a couple girls and we said it would cost $20. and hour for each one which he didn't have a problem with. So we arrange to pick up the models, take them to the camera club, they are there for 3 hours and we get a $120 check and we paid the girls the $5.00 per hour (*$15.00 they were very happy with*) so we end making $90 on the night. Back then that was terrific money. The word soon gets around that Chai-Mark Studio has some great models for Camera Clubs and we have a thriving modeling business going. One of the Models (*Windy*) was broke and asks if she can move into the Studio. (*It had a cot, full bath room and kitchenette*) In exchange she offers to be our full time secretary so how could we turn down free labor from such a cute, down on her luck, young lady. She added a great deal to the studio and she was a fanatic when it came to keeping it clean. Windy turned out to be God sent.

One weekend Paul and I decided we needed a break and elected to take a couple models up in the mountain and shoot some shots. Paul took Windy and I chose a model called Cindy, a thin, lovely girl that was a student at the University of Denver. We were just shooting cheesecake when we came upon a gnarly pine on the crest of a hill that was grotesquely beautiful. Cindy had said she would not consider posing nude, but when I explained the shot I wanted it called on her artistic side I guess and she said she agreed to "just this one." The getting her down on the rocky ground and in just the right position under the tree was hilarious. It was a series of "ouch's", "ohh's", "groans", "uggs", "upps", and "aggghs!" But it was well worth the anguish. It was totally by accident, but it just so happen, when we were taking the photo it was during a partial eclipse of the sun. The combination of the tree, the pose, the angle of the sun light and the diminished intensity but heightened quality and color of the light, composition, the tonality of the shadows, not to mention the perfect model for the scene, all combined to make it a real winner. (see picture)

A funny thing happen during the shooting of this shot. A troupe of Boy Scouts happened to march by not 30 feet from where we were shooting. They saw a real <u>bare</u> in the woods that day. The picture was reportedly the only nude to ever be a blue ribbon winner and take top honors with the Colorado Professional Photographers of America. (*at least for a great many years following, according to the son of Peter Lanson who was the President of the CPPA back in -I think- 1963*) Later when I left the Air Force and went to work for Wittenberg, a strict Lutheran University, the Vice President wanted me to have a show of my work. I asked if a nude would be appropriate and he said "Absolutely not!", but then relented enough to say "Let me see it." When he saw it he melted and said it was a beautiful work of art and I absolutely could display it, as the center piece of my work. The picture was stolen from the display, but returned many years later by a former student.

Immediately after I finished shooting the tree shot I handed Cindy her clothing and she said, "If you have some more ideas you would like to do with nude shots I'm OK with it." So we shot a few more shots, but nothing was up to the quality of the tree shot. It was soon lunch time and Windy had packed a picnic lunch for us. I believe I have said repeatedly that I am not "bothered" by shooting a nude woman, but now Cindy had become so al-la natural and suddenly loved being so free. She was running through the forest nude and singing like she was a wood nymph. She even sat down on the ground to eat her picnic lunch of cold chicken and potato salad across from me naked. Now, I have to admit, ... that did bother me. I got her a long sleeve white terrycloth robe and told her to put it on, which she did, but didn't button it. Crap, ... that was worst than wearing nothing. I ended up having to go eat my chicken else where.

Difference in Class

The name is probably not familiar now to most, but once everyone knew Sonny Liston, the Heavy Weight Boxing Champ of the world. Well, Sonny had his training camp on Lowry and during our sports photography training block of instruction I decided we could go over to his ring and shoot him sparring with one of his partners. Unfortunately, when the class arrived neither he or his entourage were there. We were about to head back when one of the troupes in the class said "Why don't you and I box and let the class shoot us." It was a young man that it was obvious he didn't particularly care for me, and everyone knew it. I was between the rock and the hard place. I couldn't back down in front of the men, but by the same token, I had never boxed in my life. He had me in both height and weight and I would guess he was an experienced fighter. What to do. I had to do it,

The Boxing Class

I had no choice. To run away I would lose the respect of all of them. The base Special Services guy got us gloves that, to my surprised, were quite padded. He ran a clock and we had actual 3 minute rounds.

The first round was a total disaster. I was nothing but a punching bag but thank God it didn't hurt nor was I knocked down. When the bell rang I went to my corner and a student from Tennessee said to me, “Have you ever boxed before Instructor Voris?” I said I hadn't. He said, “Want a suggestion?” I said, “Most definitely.” He said, “Duck! You never ducked once. You just stand there and took it! Also try hitting him!” I thought he had a couple very good ideas that I hadn't thought of yet!

The second round, I suppose my adversary was expecting me to just stand there again. He was winding up with everything he had. I think everyone in the class was prepared to shoot the shot, to be titled “The End of the Instructor” As his hay-maker was coming at me, … I ducked! Because he was in an unbalanced position I was able to give him a uppercut with everything I had. It literally lifted him off the floor and he landed on his back. Now, ... I was NOT going to lose this advantage. Be fair my ass! While he was down I was pounding on his face which was making his head bounce off the canvas. The Special Services guy is ringing the bell for me to quit, but no way, … I was going to keep it up until the guy on the floor said “I give!” He finally did and after that day the two of us got along fine. Oh, yeah, the fellow from Tennessee that gave me the boxing tips, … I made him Class Leader.

The Vietnam mess was starting up and there was the draft. As a result college guys were signing up in the Air National Guard and putting in for schools like Photography. They were way over qualified but it was an absolute joy to have them as a class. I had a class of 7 Air National Guard College kids and one poor kid out of High School that was struggling to make the grade. I could come in to class and assign the next lesson to one of the College boys, give them the curriculum materials and they would do a great job of teaching the class. They all loved doing that, it actually was a great way to teach, (*peer training*) and all I had to do was be there and occasional clear up a point or two. The only one that was struggling was the High School Student. I decided to make the class a deal. I told them that if they tutored the young man that was the High School Student through so that he made an "A" on the final, I would take the whole class down to my Studio after graduation and treat them to a party and a photo session with a nude model! That last part was all the inspiration they needed. Everyone took him under their wing and tutored him. Sure enough, he made the final with a strong "A+"

The night of graduation I had the party at the studio and Windy has volunteered to be the model. All day long the class has been going on and on about how horny they are and how they are going to have difficulty in shooting because of their anatomical anomalies' will be showing. Well as soon as Windy stepped out onto the paper background all of my fearless photographers heads dropped into the view finders and nobody said a word. I started laughing and said "Direct your model!" The High School lad was the only one that said anything and all he did was say "Turn this way a little!" Then all of a sudden the shutters were clicking like mad. Paul and I ended up lighting and directing the model. It was hilarious, they were all blow and no go.

Sorry to say that the studio was not financially viable. We were just not able to get enough commercial work to support the rent, electric, water bill and worst of all a commercial telephone bill. We had to close it up. Paul found a job in Golden as a Catholic Church Caretaker and was given a house to boot. With that he could bring Ginger and family out to Colorado. Melanie had the baby, Attiga Lee Voris and now was ready to get back together as a family unit in Denver. I was able to get our trailer put on Base which saved some money in rent.

Me a Bar Bouncer?

I got a part-time job as a bouncer at a bar in Aurora called the Zanzibar. It was used in the Movie staring Clint Eastwood "Any Which Way But Loose" It was a rough country/western bar and the owner said I was the smallest guy they ever hired as a bouncer. He was afraid I would get the "shit beat out of me!" but I wanted the job because it paid $5.00 and hour and that was a lot in 1964. I figured I'd risk it.

They put me on the front door to check ID's. A cute young lady came up to the door that had a one way mirror and just inches away was using it to put on her lipstick. When she came in I said after checking her ID, "You forgot to blot your lipstick!" She looked puzzled then realized that I was watching her through the one-way mirror and said "Okay how about I use you!" and she plants three big red lipstick kisses, two on my cheeks and one on my forehead. Pretty soon another couple girls come along and when they see me they ask, "Is that the thing to do?" I respond, "I guess so!" and they plant several more on my face and now on my shirt. Over the next few hours nearly every girl that comes in does the same and I am a red mess covered in lip stick. Guys that come in look at me say, "Man – this is the place!" (*I assume they figure if a ugly guy like me can get smother in kisses they ought to be able to do better than that!*) The place takes on a real party atmosphere and the boss loves it. He thinks its my idea and suggests we do it every night. (*Unfortunately it didn't happen again.*) At closing time (*2 a.m.*) one of the bouncers said to me, "Man are you ever going to be in trouble when you get home to your wife." I told him there would be no problem. He was foolish enough to bet me $20 that I wouldn't go home looking like I do and let my wife see me covered in lipstick. I took that bet.

We got to the trailer about 2:45 and Melanie was asleep of course. I stuck my head in and said "Put your house coat on and come out to the kitchen, I have to show you something, it is important!" After a few minutes sleep eyed Melanie comes dragging her tail out to the kitchen and sees me. The first words she said is, "Looks like there was a good time at the Zanzibar tonight." The bouncer looking at me shaking his head said "Jeez, I don't believe it, by ol' lady would be screaming at me. I wouldn't believe it if I didn't see it. Here is your $20." and he left. Melanie said, "What was that all about?" I answered, "Trust sweetheart, trust!"

Another time I am at the door there is a wrestling convention in Denver. There is one of these "wrestlers" alone in a booth. In order for it to accommodate him, he has had to push the table all the way to the opposite side, because he takes up the whole seat. He is a mammoth man. Unfortunately it is still early and I am the only "bouncer" in the bar. Our giant guest is being obnoxious and shouting obscenities and the manager (*5foot 2inches about 120 lbs*) said to me to "Throw him out!"

I am not sure if you remember if I mentioned the part about him being HUGE and me being the smallest bouncer the bar ever had. Now we all have heard the story of David and Goliath but my name is Jim and while he may well fit the name I seriously doubt if his name was Goliath. Besides I never used a sling in my life and it is a little late to learn now. It is time for me to use all my tactical skills which does NOT include any form of martial arts. I proceeded to his table and upon arrival I start to laugh. I laugh so hard I drop my head to his table on my arm. He said, in a voice that sounds like the giant in "*Jack and the Bean Stock*" reciting *Fe fie foe fum*!, "What the hell are you laughing at pip squeak?"

I straighten up and through my laughing say, "Can you see that little guy standing up by the door?" He responds with a "yes!" " I continue, "Well, (*Ha! Ha!*) He is the manager and I, (*pshupsss! ... More laughter*) and I … am the bouncer and He told me to … get this, told me to THROW YOU OUT! Ha ha ha!" I got tears in my eyes from laughing. (*not really – more from fear!*)

The wrestler looks at the manager with contempt and then at me. He then said in a soft voice not much above a whisper, "Okay, here is what we are going to do. When I come up out of the booth you grab my hand and put it behind my back. I'll drop to one knee and we'll work our way out the door. You keep holding my hand behind my back, got it?

"What?" I say.

"Just follow my lead." Then suddenly he shouts at the top of his lungs that everyone in the bar looks to see what is going on. "You are going to do what you little fuckin pipsqueek!" He stands up and in the process the table in his booth pushes the booth in front of him about a foot and that knocks the folks in that booth into their booth knocking everything over. He reached out for my throat and as he grabbed it said in a low voice,

"Grab my hand, grab my hand!"

Now let me explain something at this juncture. The wrist of that monster was about the diameter of my knee so it took two hands to go partially around and when I did - he, not I, twirled his arm around behind him and I practically flew through the air to keep up with it. I had to do everything in my power to just hold on. Once behind him (*as promised*) he went down on one knee and bellowed like a wounded buffalo. If I didn't know better I would believe I was seriously damaging this hulk. He was trashing his one free arm around acting like he was trying to reach me as we kept making small two foot movements toward the door. Tables were being pushed and chairs tossed from our path. The bar was dead silent as we finally exited. Once out front he stood up, winked, brushed himself off and said, "How's that, champ?" Jesus, what a performance!

I waited a minute or so for my heart to finally restart and settle to a universally accepted beat. As I did so I watched my benefactor stagger off down the street. Upon reentered the bar the place went wild with cheers and clapping. The boss was still in shock and said, shaking his head, "In all my years in this business, I ain't never seen nothin like that before!" I neglected to tell them him really happen. Not on your life.

There were only two times I ever had an actual altercation with a bar customer. In both cases they were small guys, smaller than me. One was in a booth and drunk shouting obscenities and the boss said throw him out. I went back and politely asked him to leave. He said he couldn't get up. He was sitting in a booth that was next to the door to the kitchen so I could get directly behind him. I was helping him out when all of a sudden he tried to hit me. Well, first of all I was behind and above him and second he is drunk and uncoordinated. I dropped him back in the booth and tell him to stop that. He said "Okay!" I asked him if he needed help in getting up? He said yes and once again I'm behind him lifting and he tried to hit me. I drop him again and tell him to settle down and am holding his hands from hitting me. The manager comes back and said, "Let him go." I say, "He wants to hit someone." The manager was standing right in front of him and said to me "Let him go!" I do and, ... POW, ... the drunk slugged the manager square in the mouth sending him across the table and knocked him on his keaster. He got up holding his mouth and mumbles "Throw the S.O.B. out!" Now I pull him out of the booth and as he keeps trying to hit me I keep tossing him back on the floor. He finally tired of this and with an arm lock we navigate through the bar to the front door where he is released. Upon returning his girlfriend announces that he has a gun in the car and said he was going to get it. Enough of that. I called the Aurora Police that two cars pulled up in front just as he was walking up to the bar carrying his gun. I saw from the door one way mirror, the police take down. They were not gentle. I understand he got six months for that little mistake.

The only other altercation was also a little guy. It started when a bar maid came running up to me saying some guy was on the dance floor with a knife. I only have my flashlight (*for checking I.D.'s*) but I run out anyway. There is this shrimp of a guy holding a switch blade knife like he's something out of "West Side Story" saying "I'm gonna cut somebody!" I said, "No, now, no, you're not, buddy. Come on, you don't want to do this. Why don't you just give me the knife and lets go over to the bar." Unfortunately, he was adamant about wanting to "Cut somebody!" and kept waving it around. The way he was holding it was clutched in his right hand, his thumb extended along the knife's back (*dull*) edge. His knuckles were up and an open invitation for me to whack them with my flash light. Which I did and when I did his hand automatically sprang open, the knife fell to the dance floor. I stepped on the blade and pulled on the handle sideways, braking the blade off, handing him the blade-less handle. He is yelling, "You broke my fuckin hand, you broke my fuckin knife!" He is holding his hand and his broken knife and he keeps repeating this over and over as I escorted him out the door. I got another round of applause from the bar patrons on that one too! But the boss wasn't that impressed.

Another way I had in making a buck was to walk down the street and shoot pictures of store fronts. Then I would print an 8x10 and go back to each store and see if I could sell the Manager/Owner the print for a Dollar. It was always a sure sell. At one barber shop the owner said, pointing to his wall, "I am an amateur photographer and as you can see I have several shots of this place on the wall." I said I understood and as I was leaving he said, "Awe what the heck, for a buck. Your picture is better than mine anyway, I'll take it!"

We were honored to have a real hero as the top sergeant at the Photo School, SM/Sgt Clyde Scarbough. He was the first Chief Master and first Senior Master Sergeant to be awarded those ranks in the Air Force when they were first became authorized. During WWII he was in the European Theater and was a prisoner of war three times, and escaped twice, liberated the third time. He was one of the finest men I have ever had the privilege to have served with. It was fun to sit in the Instructor lounge and hear some of his stories. I was proud to see his uniform is displayed at Wright Patterson AFB in the US Air Force Museum. That makes two items at that museum that I have a personal connection to. *(SM/Sgt Clyde Scarbough and the "Lady Be Good" and the whole Wheelus Base Chapel stain-glass window display)*

Then Full-Time Part-time Work

I was approaching the last 6 months of my enlistment. Nobody was getting promoted, all ranks were "frozen" (*meaning there were no spaces to promote to in our career field*) and they wanted me to go to NCO academy. This was a glorified Basic Training refresher course. Recall that I mentioned Vietnam was heating up and the draft had been started. The real kicker for me was they started sending our graduates to a Combat Photography School with the Army to give them extended training in ground combat photo experience. That convinced me it was time to become a civilian. I had all my military commitment completed so there was no chance of being drafted and besides Melanie wanted to "go home." So I chose to not go to the NCO School. Now the Military does not particularly like it's troupes saying "no" even when you add "thank you." I was called before the Squadron Commander who said, quote, "You WILL go to NCO School or you WILL go to the brig." I responded, "Well Sir, I guess I can write my Congressman from the Brig and tell him how all I am trying to do was save the Air Force money, because I am most definitely not reenlisting." He was doing a slow burn, his face was red and said, "You better not reenlist. Get out of my site!" I salute, did an about face and exited. Now everyone gets numerous counseling sessions trying to convince you to re-up, (*reenlist*) but I didn't, NOT ONE!

I left the Zanzibar bouncer job to take a job with Frito Lay in Denver, as a janitor. They were also paying $5.00 an hour but more hours than I could get at the bar. At Frito Lay it was a full 8 hours 6 days a week so you even got 8 hours at time and a half . The hours were terrible though because it had to be a night shift (*3 to midnight*) and I was still working at 6am to 2:30p.m. at the base. Lucky it was about 20 minutes from the base so I was seldom late. (*But exhausted getting often 4 hours sleep a night)* To get hired you had to take an entry test consisting of tough questions like 1. A Cow goes (a)- Bow Wow (b)- Baaaa (c)- Mooo or (d)- Cocka doo doodle do . The math portion was equally hard with questions like 1. An item cost $2.85 and is offered at a 25% discount. This means : (a) you pay more than $2.85 (b) you pay less than $2.85 (c) you pay exactly $2.85 (d) you don't have enough information to accurately answer this question or answer not given. Apparently I passed and was given the job. In an effort to stay awake I kept myself busy. If I wasn't sweeping, I was emptying trash or potato scrap bins, or cleaning down the lines that were not in use. I looked for something to keep me busy. After a couple weeks the night plant manager comes up to me and said "I've been watching you and I'm impressed. How would you like to run the forklift in the warehouse, it pays $5.50 an hour." "Sure!" I say, "Whatever you want me to do, but I advised him that I never operated a forklift before." He told me they would train me so off to the warehouse I go. My GOD! It is a mammoth, cold dark place that all you did every half hour or so was bring a huge bin of potatoes to a lift. Get off your forklift and press a button that turned the bin over and dumped the potatoes into a hopper. From there they were fed automatically into the plant. The only job of the forklift operator was to make sure the hopper always had potatoes. So once trained, (*a 15 minute job*) I am alone in this cavernous (*did I mention dark*) place. I have to fight staying awake. What to do, what to do? I notice that the big bins have dates on them. I also notice that apparently when they are delivered (*in the day*) the day shift guys just put the new arrivals in front of the older potatoes. I think this is bad business, the stock should be first in first out. So I start reshuffling the stock putting the newest in the back and oldest up front. The next bin I put in is one of the oldest. A week goes by and the Night Plant Manager came back to visit me. He asks me what I'm doing, as I am busily zooming around in the warehouse. I tell him I am shuffling the stock in order that the oldest is used first. "Ahh, that explains it!" he said. "When you first came back here our quality control went to hell, we were making potato-chips for XYZ companies and then it started leveling off. Now it is the most consistent it has been in years. Rotating the stock huh? Very good. How would you like to be a quality control line inspector? It pays $6.00 an hour?" "Sure!" I say having no idea what a quality control line inspector is.

Imagine this. There are two 15 foot long two foot in diameter drums with sharp barbs that are on an incline flushed with water. Potato's are then fed down this tube to be peeled and washed. Now stark white potato's are dumped out on a series of black rollers with little nubs that are turning to keep the potato's moving along at about the same rate that Lucy an Ethel have found challenging at the chocolate factory. Now the job of the quality control line inspector was to grab any rotten potato or cut out any rotten portion of a potato. A rotten portion is brown (*or black if real bad*) and after just five minutes of standing in front of this sea of white specks moving across a black field with an occasional brown one you are totally hypnotized. It is like staring at a TV screen that isn't tuned to a channel and all you see is the snow, the little white specks against a black background. I didn't make it through one night before, at the first break, I found the Night Manager and told him the problem. "Paint the rollers the same color as the potato's. Then all you will see is the rotten portions." I suffered through that first night, but the next night they were painted and it was very easy to do the job. The quality went through the roof. The suggestion went up the corporation ladder and was, to the best of my knowledge, instituted corporate wide. I was only a quality control line inspector a few more nights and the Night Shift Plant Manager came to me saying he would like me to be the Line Inspector. This was a big jump to $8.00 an hour and all I had to do was keep the line going. This was a piece of cake. I loved this job. Nothing is quite as good as the taste of a potato chip as it comes hot out of the oil and right after the salter. About the only suggestion I can be credited with there is potato chips that are bagged and rejected because they were underweight were ripped open and dumped in a barrel and sold to pig farmers for pennies. I suggested that a certain number be put in boxes and set by the time clock so that employees as they clocked out could take as many as they wanted. It was very popular and I understand it also went Frito Lay wide. My time was up and I was about to get out of the Air Force so I turned in my two week notice to the Plant Manager. He called me into his Office. "I am glad to hear you are about to get out of the Air Force Jim, but I don't understand why you are leaving us. You have a fantastic career ahead here. We have been watching you ever since you came aboard and aced the entrance exam. (*I think he was talking about the Cow goes Moo test!*) Your progress and suggestions have been outstanding. I promise you that you can be the Night Shift Manager within 3 months and have your own Plant within another year after that." I looked at him and thanked him profusely but used my wife as the excuse we had to go back to Ohio. What I really was thinking "I really don't think I'd like making potato chips the rest of my life."

Getting Short

Once I got so short in my time left that their wasn't sufficient enlistment time to take a class through a full cycle, they put me in charge of Chem mix and the lab darkroom block. All I had to do was supervise some recruits to mix huge vats of chemicals and to keep the labs clean. It was a

"not do much" job. As a result I wrote up a couple suggestions on ways the AF could save some money, not expecting any response because they were such "dah – yah sure- but of course!" things. The next month just as I am getting out I receive a check for $200 as a suggestion award. (*Note: Nothing was ever said about the laser idea, but several years later I saw a device on an aircraft's tail that a swear looked like it was a laser. I often wondered what ever happen with that research?*)

With only days to go Melanie and I had sold the trailer and we moved off Base. We moved in with Paul and Ginger who had just bought a new house in Thornton, north of Denver. Paul and I were horsing around and wrestling. I always beat Paul when we wrestled because all I had to do was start tickling him in the arm pits and he would go crazy. He was coming at me in a hallway and I put my foot up to his chest height. (*I could* ***do*** *that in those days!*) Paul grabbed my foot and took off running holding my foot. There I was bouncing down the hall on one foot until I come to a throw rug on the hardwood floor which promptly slid out from under my foot and I came crashing down. My head landed with a bang and that was the last thing I remember until hours later. I then recall we were playing cards and I started waving my hands around and complaining that I could only see in this small tunnel. It was soon evident I was experiencing tunnel vision and had at least a minor concussion. Melanie decided to take me to Fitsimmons Military Hospital, where the Doctor explicitly told Melanie NOT to say anything to the question he was going to ask. His first question, "What is your address?" Having just moved to Paul's I really didn't know the address, I knew how to get there but not the address, so I said, "I, … I don't know the address but," and before I can explain he asks "What is your phone number?" Same situation and before I can explain he asks "Do you know what happen to you?" Now you have to realize that when you have a bunch of kids you answer some questions in the manner they understand without thinking about who is asking and I responded, "I fall down and go boom!" Melanie is trying to butt-in to explain but he is shushing her and looking at me like he finally has a case that he can write up in the Psychology Today Medical Journals. He said "I think we need to put him in overnight for observation and make sure he hasn't suffered any lasting brain damage. I think it is just a mild concussion, but let's just make sure. So off to the ward I go. The nurse asks me when I got up to go to the bathroom where I was going. I responded "I gotta go to the potty!" (*Damn I kept forgetting where I was!*) She said she was going with me. I said, "Ohh no your not." She said "Then I will be outside the door here so you better hurry." Boy that was the fastest pee in history!

The next day a guy from an investigating office came around to see me and asked, "Were you in a bar when this fight broke out?" "What?" I said, "No, first there was no fight and we weren't in any bar, I was staying at my friends house with my family and we were just horsing around." He said "How much did you have to drink?" I said "I wasn't drinking, ... anything, not even a soda." Then he said, "What was your friend drinking?" I was getting a bit upset at this point and said, "Look damn it. I told you we were just horsing around. He is my best friend. He hadn't had anything to drink, I hadn't had anything to drink, we were just wrestling. Don't you have any friends you wrestle with? It is just friendly horse play. Generally I get him down and tickle him and he gives up, this time I tripped and bumped my head. Got it?" He then said, "Are you guys homo's" "What!" I shout, "I am there with my wife and three kids with his wife and four kids. They are kind enough to put us up for a couple of days before I get out of the Air Force. Get out of my sight! You make me sick." Later I got a report that said "After a cursory investigation, it was determined that no charges would be brought or time lost as a result of the altercation between the off duty service personnel and a civilian that took place in the home of the civilian."

Well - I'm Unemployed

But BS is Good!

I had sent out many Resume's but only received two responses. One positive return from the International Harvester Company indicated they wanted to see me as soon as I arrived in Springfield. The other was from Wittenberg University that, while courteous said "We will place you Resume on file." and really was only an acknowledge they received my correspondence. No one else in 40 resumes sent even acknowledge receipt.

Upon arrival in our home town of Springfield, Ohio, the very next day I contacted the Personnel Office at International Harvester and they set me up to interview the very next day. This was encouraging and I figured I had it made. The International Harvester Company was the cities largest employer and had great benefits. I dress for the position and was 5 minutes ahead of time for my appointment. The interview was a slam dunk. They were impressed with my credentials and background and seemed to like me. Then they wanted to know how soon I would be able to go to Fort Wayne, Indiana? What? But you don't understand. We moved back to Springfield, my family, my wife's family were here. They apologized but said their big commercial photo facilities were in Fort Wayne and that is where I was needed. They said I was way over qualified for the Springfield Plant's photography needs. I left the meeting crushed, convinced that now the family and I were going to starve to death and getting out of the Air Force was really a bad idea.

I decided that I had lots of time so I might as well call on the only other place that at least responded to my resume, Wittenberg College (*It wasn't a University yet*) I found the Personnel Office and got to see the Assistant Director of Personnel. We had a lovely chat and at the conclusion he said "I am sorry, but the College uses Students to shoot all of the pictures it needs for it's publications and news releases." I responded with, "Oh, well I guess if the College is willing to let it's image be represented by students who am I to say." He looks at me a moment and said, "Can you wait just a moment, I'd like you to talk to the Director of Personnel." I have no where else to go so "Sure!" I am taken into the the Director's office who is a real peach of a guy. We talk for a good half hour then he finally said something like, "It's too bad, but the College uses its students to shoot pictures it needs for the various publications and news releases." I again respond with "Oh, well I suppose if the College wants it's image be represented by students who am I to say." He looks at me and said, "Your right. Do you have time to talk to someone else. I would like you to meet the Vice President, Dr. Emerson Reck. He is in charge of Public Relations and is who you really should be talking to." He picks up the phone and in a matter of minutes I am delivered upstairs to the Vice Presidents Office. After introductions I have another wonderful conversation with Dr. Reck and again it concludes with his saying that they use Students for all their photographic needs. It has worked for me twice before so one more time I whip it on Dr. Reck. "Oh, well I guess if the College is willing to let it's image be controlled by students viewpoints who am I to say." He looked at me for a moment and said, You know you make a good point. We are becoming a University and it just so happens that all my good student photographers are graduating. (*this was in late May*) How much do you want. (*I had no preparation time to think this out.*) "I don't think I could get by on less than $100 a week." I stupidly said. He said, "Okay, that is $2.50 an hour. I'll hire you at that rate and we'll see where it goes. I have need of a picture in our new computer center down stairs. The New Director of the center and his staff standing with the machines. Do you think you could shoot that tomorrow?" "Yes Sir!" I said. The next morning I came in with my 4x5 camera and big strobe. I posed them and as I was ready to shoot the Director of the Computer Center said, "Sir, excuse me, but your flash is pointing up."

"Yes, I know, It's called bounce flash. It makes a very soft light, you'll like it!" I shot the pictures, immediately went to the schools darkroom, processed the film and even printed the best negative wet. Fourth-five minutes later I dropped off a print to the Director of the Computer Center for his approval which he about crapped his pants over. He raved and raved on and on about it. Then I ran a couple more 8x10 copies up to Dr. Reck's Office. He couldn't believe it. He was used to waiting two weeks chasing after his student photographers to get fuzzy pictures. He kept looking at the prints, marveling at their sharpness and how fast it was. I told him it would have been faster but I stopped to get the Director of the Computer Center's approval before I brought them up. This also impressed Dr. Reck immensely. Suddenly Dr. Reck was having me shoot everything. In fact the first week he worked me 80 hours and the second week 60 hours. When he brought me my first pay check he said, "From now on you are full time Staff and Salary." I was at Wittenberg 13 years 6 years as the photographer then 7 years as the Director of Audio Visual Services. I taught through the Art Department Photography and

Audio Visual Courses in both the Day school and Evening School. I started at $5,200.year and after 13 years was still only making $13,000 annual. Wittenberg was not a place to get rich monetarily, but thanks to Dr. Emerson Reck, he put me on TIAA-CREF retirement from day one and I actually have drawn more from my retirement from Wittenberg than I ever earned from working there.

Well, that's the story. I had the joy of being called at odd hours and asked, "Are you the Mr. Voris that taught at Wittenberg University, or Clark Technical College, or District One Technical Institute, or Hennepin Technical College?" and told things like "I just wanted to tell you how much of an influence you had on my life." Or "I wanted to thank you for all the things you opened my life to." One call, at supper time, I thought was a phone marketer until they said, "I just wanted to tell you I was filling out my taxes and discovered that, for the first time, I made over $100,000 profit this year and I attribute it to the principles you taught to us. Thank you Mr. Voris." I went back to my meal (*and guest*) with big tears in my eyes.

I realize I am not, ever was, or ever will become, a great photographer. My images will never hang in the galleries next to the greats like Ansel Adams, Annie Leibovitz, Alfred Stieglitz, or such. But just maybe, the works of one, or more, of the many thousands of students I have had the privilege to tutelage over the years – just may. That would mean infinitely so much more to me than anything I could ever produce. To me it would mean that a tiny, tiny part of me would survive, no matter how obscure or unidentified. Maybe, just maybe they may remember their old Instructor. That's what is important, not my accomplishments, but theirs.

I hope you enjoyed my adventures as much as I still do. - Jim Voris

The First Time I met God. A modern tale of intrigue with twists and turns to make you hold on tight. A man's free-willed choice to by-pass a traffic jam, sets a chain of events that people are unaware of their part until years later. The first decision is one of life or death. Can Jim let go his hold on life in order to live? Decisions thread their way through the book, coming to a critical happening in 2014. Shouldn't the event, the Virgin Birth by Immaculate Conception, and the coming of a Messiah astound the world? But, despite using the most advanced equipment, the proof is shown only to the world's top Religious leaders. The Virgin mother, Sara, delivers a GIRL with immense powers like the Christ before her, the child must be taught how to channel and use them to the better good. But is this child here to save the world, or is she the anti-Christ? If you guess the ending, you are truly one in a million! You'll want to laugh out loud, shed a tear, and be there with them in their incredible talks with God.

The Waters - Book 1 "The Valley" Geo is a handsome 25-year-old Italian want-a-be aristocrat of 1465 that pines for a chance to trade in the riches of the Far East. An old Arab offers him a secret map to China that is his chance to gain wealth and power. The map is his special ticket to an incredible valley, where life is extended thousands of years. He finds a fantastic love awaits, beyond anything he can imagine and in fourteen short years he fathers thousands of children. He learns to understand life, love and passion beyond the possessive, hurtful, demanding nature of "love" in the outside world. But, the gift of extended life carries a big price. As they drink "The Waters" all gradually become sterile. Aliens are the true reason for the sterility as well as extended life, but the aliens never came across a planet where sex is a means of procreation and they too must learn to co-exist in an open symbiotic relationship. Follow Geo in this thought stimulating and exciting sensual adventure in a place called "The Valley." [*Warning – intended for Adult audiences only*]

The Waters - Book 2 "Contact"The aliens need to make contact if they are to help the Valley people overcome the infertility problem they created when giving the humans greatly extended life. Geo and Wan Za are selected to be the first contacts but it means breaking the ancient rules and even messing with the prime directive of no interference with "free will." It works, but what hath they created,... children that are too perfect,... that are millions of years beyond us on the evolutionary scale. [*Warning – intended for Adult audiences only*]

Tra$h Man This is a fun tale that takes place in the not so distant future about the misadventures of a highly imaginative, nerdy old guy, named Harry B. Mills. Through inheritance he uses his fortunes to finance his dream invention, a matter-transmitter. He did it, and in the process became unbelievably wealthy. But alas, unknowingly, his process created a 'singularity' every time it operated. They all began to attract to each other and slowly sank to the gravitational center of the earth. Once there, they became a black hole. Harry's invention was eating the whole planet from the inside out, creating the unstoppable end of the Earth. The adventure then shifts to how the tormented, guilt-ridden Harry, with the help of three dear friends, attempts to save the mankind he accidentally doomed. The reader is woven into a series of paradoxical situations of how Harry and his inventions make him the most hated man in the Galaxy. So hated he has to take his 'recorded' mass of humanity to our closest neighboring Galaxy, Andromeda. There he encounters an Alien race that 'know him' and admonish him for leaving the safety of his home on Centheea. Join Harry and his three friends on this wild ride across the cosmos. You'll never guess the ending and will be amazed at the many concepts and inventions presented designed to make you think.

Note: All listed books are available in Hard Bound, Soft Cover, E- Book Form (IE: Kindle/Sony/Etc.) or computer download. (Adobe Reader)

You are welcome and encouraged to contact the Author to give your constructive comments or critique of this book at:

jim.voris@yahoo.com

Visit the Authors website at

www.jamesleevorisbooks.com

and be up on all the latest book release.